THE MILK TRAIN DOESN'T STOP HERE ANYMORE

"Consume my heart away; sick with desire
And fastened to a dying animal
It knows not what it is; and gather me
Into the artifice of eternity."
—FROM *Sailing to Byzantium*
BY WILLIAM BUTLER YEATS

By TENNESSEE WILLIAMS

PLAYS

Baby Doll (a screenplay)
Cat on a Hot Tin Roof
The Glass Menagerie
The Night of the Iguana
Orpheus Descending
Period of Adjustment
The Rose Tattoo
A Streetcar Named Desire
Suddenly Last Summer
Summer and Smoke
Three Plays
    The Rose Tattoo
    Camino Real
    Sweet Bird of Youth
27 Wagons Full of Cotton and Other Plays

POETRY

In the Winter of Cities

PROSE

The Roman Spring of Mrs. Stone
One Arm and Other Stories
Hard Candy and Other Stories

THE MILK TRAIN DOESN'T STOP HERE ANYMORE

by TENNESSEE WILLIAMS

A NEW DIRECTIONS BOOK

1964

AUTHOR'S NOTES

Sometimes theatrical effects and devices such as those I have adopted in the third (and I hope final) version of this play are ascribed to affectation or "artiness," so it may be helpful for me to explain a bit of my intention in the use of these effects and devices, and let the play's production justify or condemn them.

I have added to the cast a pair of stage assistants that function in a way that's between the Kabuki Theatre of Japan and the chorus of Greek theatre. My excuse, or reason, is that I think the play will come off better the further it is removed from conventional theatre, since it's been rightly described as an allegory and as a "sophisticated fairy tale."

Stage assistants in Japanese Kabuki are a theatrical expedient. They work on stage during the performance, shifting set pieces, placing and removing properties and furniture. Now and then in this play they have lines to speak, very short ones that serve as cues to the principal performers. . . . They should be regarded, therefore, as members of the cast. They sometimes take a balletic part in the action of the play. They should be dressed in black, very simply, to represent invisibility to the other players. The other players should never appear to see them, even when they speak or take part in the action, except when they appear "in costume."

THE SETTING represents the library and bedroom of the white villa, downstage, and the bedrooms of the pink and blue villinos: most importantly, the terrace of the white villa, I think, should extend the whole width of the proscenium, with a small apron for a white iron bench, a step down from the terrace.

1

Separations between interior and exterior should not be clearly defined except by lighting. When a single interior is being used, the other interior areas should be masked by light, folding screens, painted to blend with the cyclorama, that is, in sea-and-sky colors: they should be set in place and removed by the stage assistants. The cyclorama and these folding screens represent, preferably in a semi-abstract style, the mountain-sea-sky of Italy's Divina Costiera *in summer.*

Since the villas are, naturally, much farther apart than they can appear on the stage, the director could adopt a convention of having actors, who are to go from one villa to another, make their exits into the wings. They would wait till the stage assistants have removed the screens that mask the next interior to be used, and then come back out and enter that area.

August, 1963.

THE MILK TRAIN DOESN'T STOP HERE ANYMORE

THE PLAYERS

MRS. GOFORTH

CHRISTOPHER FLANDERS

BLACKIE

THE WITCH OF CAPRI

RUDY, a watchman

GIULIO

SIMONETTA

TWO STAGE ASSISTANTS
  (Sometimes appearing in
  costume for small parts)

MEMBERS OF THE KITCHEN STAFF

PROLOGUE

At the rise of the curtain, the STAGE ASSISTANTS *are on stage. All the interior areas are masked by their individual screens. The light of the cyclorama suggests early dawn.*

ONE: Daybreak: flag-raising ceremony on Mrs. Goforth's mountain.

TWO: Above the oldest sea in the Western world.

ONE: Banner.

[TWO *hands it to him.* TWO *places the staff in a socket near the right wings and attaches the flag to it. A fan in the wings whips it out as it is being raised, so that the audience can see the device on it clearly.*]

ONE: The device on the banner is a golden griffin.

TWO: A mythological monster, half lion, and half eagle.

ONE: And completely human.

TWO: Yes, wholly and completely human, that's true.

ONE: We are also a device.

TWO: A theatrical device of ancient and oriental origin.

ONE: With occidental variations, however.

TOGETHER: We are Stage Assistants. We move the screens that mask the interior playing areas of the stage presentation.

ONE: We fetch and carry.

TWO: Furniture and props.

ONE: To make the presentation—the play or masque or pageant—move more gracefully, quickly through the course of the two final days of Mrs. Goforth's existence.

5

MRS. GOFORTH'S VOICE [*offstage; half sleeping*]: Ahhhhhhhh, Meeeeeeeeee . . .

[*There is heard the sound of distant church bells.*]

ONE: The actors will not seem to hear us except when we're in costume.

TWO: They will never see us, except when we're in costume.

ONE: Sometimes we will give them cues for speech and participate in the action.

MRS. GOFORTH'S VOICE [*off stage*]: Ahhhhhhh, Ahhhhhh, Ahhhhhh . . .

[ONE *and* TWO *show no reaction to this human cry.*]

MRS. GOFORTH'S VOICE [*off stage; more wakefully*]: Another day, Oh, Christ, Oh, Mother of Christ!

[*There is silence, a pause, as the cyclorama's lighting indicates the progress of the day toward the meridian.*]

ONE *and* TWO [*together*]: Our hearts are invisible, too.

[*The fan that whipped out the flag bearing the personal emblem, the griffin, of* MRS. GOFORTH, *dies down and the flag subsides with it, and will not whip out again till the flag-lowering ceremony which will take place during the last three lines of the play.*]

[*Now it is noon. Electric buzzers sound from various points on the stage. The* STAGE ASSISTANTS *cross rapidly up center and remove a screen, the middle panel of which is topped by* MRS. GOFORTH'S *heraldic device, the gold griffin. The library of the white villa is unmasked and the play begins.*]

SCENE ONE

MRS. GOFORTH *and her secretary,* BLACKIE, *are on stage.*

MRS. GOFORTH: I made my greatest mistake when I put a fast car in his hands, that red demon sports car, his fighting cock, I called it, which he drove insanely, recklessly, between my estate and the Casino at Monte Carlo, so recklessly that the Police Commissioner of Monaco came personally to ask me. Correction, *beg* me. Correction, *implore* me!— To insist that he go with me in the Rolls with a chauffeur at the wheel, as a protection of his life and of the lives of others.— M. le Commissionaire, I said, for me there are no others.— I know, Madame, he said, but for the others there are others.— Then I confessed to the Commissioner of Police that over this young poet with Romanov blood in his veins, I had no more control than my hands had over the sea-wind or the storms of the sea. At night he had flying dreams, he would thrash his arms like wings, and once his hand, on which he wore a signet ring with the heavy Romanov crest, struck me in the mouth and drew blood. After *that, necessarily*—twin beds . . .

BLACKIE: Mrs. Goforth, excuse me, but the last thing I have typed up is—oh, here it is.— "My first two husbands were ugly as apes and my third one resembled an ostrich."— Now if this passage you're dictating to me comes in direct sequence it will sound as if you had put the fast car in the hands of the ostrich.

[*There is a long, tempestuous pause.*]

MRS. GOFORTH: Aren't you the sly one, oh, you're sly as ten flies when you want to give me the needle, aren't you, Miss Blackie? My first three marriages were into Dun and Bradstreet's and the Social Register, both!— My first husband, Harlon Goforth, whose name I still carry after three later marriages— that dignified financier, *tycoon!*—was a man that Presidents

7

put next to their wives at banquets in the White House, and you sit there smoking in my face, when you know I've been told to quit smoking, and you make a joke of my work with a dead-pan expression on your Vassar-girl face, in your Vassar-girl voice, and *I will not tolerate it!*— You know goddamn well I'm talking about my *fourth* husband, the *last* one, the one I married for love, who plunged off the Grande Corniche between Monte Carlo and—died that night in my arms in a clinic at Nice: and my heart died with him! Forever! [*Her voice breaks.*]

BLACKIE: I'm sorry, Mrs. Goforth. [*Puts out cigarette.*] I'm no writer but I do think in writing there has to be some kind of logical—sequence, continuity—between one bit and the next bit, and the last thing you dictated to me—

MRS. GOFORTH: Was it something I put on the tape-recorder in my bedroom after I'd been given one of those injections that upset my balance at night?

BLACKIE: I took it off your bedroom tape this morning.

MRS. GOFORTH: Always check those night recordings with me before we begin to work the following morning. We're working against time, Blackie. Remember, try to remember, I've got two deadlines to meet, my New York publishers and my London publishers, both, have my memoirs on their Fall List. I said fall. It's already late in August. Now do you see why there's no time for goofing, or must I draw you a picture of autumn leaves falling?

BLACKIE: Mrs. Goforth, I think those publishers' deadlines are unrealistic, not to say cruel, and as for me, I not only have to function as a secretary but as an *editor*, I have to *collate* the material you dictate to me and I'm not being sly or cruel, I'm just being *honest* with you when I tell you—

MRS. GOFORTH [*cutting in*]: All cruel people describe themselves as paragons of frankness!

8

BLACKIE: I think we'd better stop now.

MRS. GOFORTH: *I* think we'd better go *on,* now!

BLACKIE: Mrs. Goforth, the Police Commissioner of Monaco was right when he told you that there were "others." I am one of those "others." I've had no sleep, scarcely any at all and—

MRS. GOFORTH: *You've* had no sleep? What about me, how much sleep do *I* get?

BLACKIE: You sleep till noon or after!

MRS. GOFORTH: Under sedation, with nightmares!

BLACKIE: Your broker is on the phone . . .

[*The* STAGE ASSISTANTS *have entered with phone.*]

MRS. GOFORTH [*immediately brightening*]: Chuck, baby, how're we doing? Ah-huh, glamour stocks still slipping? Don't hold on to 'em, dump them before they drop under what I bought 'em at, baby. We'll start buying back when they hit the basement level.— Don't give me an argument, Sell! Sell! Hell!— It's building into a crash! So, baby, I'm hitting the silk! High, low, jack and the game! Ho ho!

[*She bangs down the phone, exhilarated, and it is removed by one of the* STAGE ASSISTANTS. *The other* ASSISTANT *has rushed to the stage-right wings, and he now appears in a white doctor's jacket. This is one of the costumes that make the* ASSISTANTS *seen and heard by the other actors.*]

ASSISTANT [*as* DR. LULLO]: *Buon giorno!*

MRS. GOFORTH: What's he wheeling in here that looks like a baby-buggy for a baby from Mars?

[*He is pushing a "mock-up" of a portable X-ray machine.*]

BLACKIE: It's something your doctor in Rome, Dr.—what? Rengucci?—had sent up here to spare you the trouble of inter-

9

rupting your work to take a new set of pictures to show what progress there is in the healing of the lesion, the lung abscess, that—

MRS. GOFORTH: Oh, so you're having private consultations with that quack in Rome?

BLACKIE: Just routine calls that he told me to make sure to spare you the trouble of—

MRS. GOFORTH: Spare me no trouble, just spare me your goddamn *presumptions!*

DR. LULLO: *Forse più tardi, forse un po' più tardi?*

MRS. GOFORTH: Will you get your sneaky grin out of here? *Va, va. Presto!*

[*He retires quickly from the lighted area.* MRS. GOFORTH *advances both fearfully and threateningly upon the medical apparatus.*]

My outside is public, but my insides are private, and the Rome quack was hired by my bitch daughter that wants to hang black crepe on me. Wants to know if I'm going, and when I'll go. Doesn't know that if and when I do go, she gets one dollar, the rest goes to a—a *cultural foundation!*—named for *me!* Blackie, wheel this thing off the terrace, to the cliff-side of the mountain and shove it over!

BLACKIE: Mrs. Goforth, you mustn't ask me to do ridiculous things.

MRS. GOFORTH: I don't do ridiculous things and don't ask anyone else to do 'em for me. But if you think it's ridiculous of me to show my opinion of Rengucci's presumption and—*Look, watch this! Here we go, perambulator from Mars. Out, down, go!*

10

[*She thrusts it violently onto the forestage, where it is seized by the* STAGE ASSISTANTS *and rushed into the wings. She crosses onto the forestage, leaning forward to watch its fall off the cliff. After a couple of moments, we hear a muted crash that signifies its destruction on the rocky beach under the mountain. Then she straightens, dizzily, with a fierce laugh, and staggers back toward the library area, where* BLACKIE, *meanwhile, has closed her notebook and rushed off stage. Heartbeat sounds are heard amplified, as* MRS. GOFORTH *moves distractedly about the library area, calling out breathlessly for* BLACKIE. *She presses several buttons on the "intercom" box on the desk: electric buzzers sound from here and there on the stage but no one responds: She washes down a pill with a swig of brandy. The heart-beat sounds subside as her agitation passes. She sinks into the desk chair.*]

Ahhh . . .

[*She activates her tape-recorder and speaks into it with a voice that is plaintively childlike.*]

Blackie, the boss is sorry she took her nerves out on you. It's those night injections I take for my—neuralgia—neuritis—bursitis. The pick-up pills and the quiet-down pills: nerves shot . . .

[*A sea wave booms under the mountain.*]

Oh, God, Blackie, I'm *scared!* You know what I'm scared of? Possibly, maybe, the Boss is—dying this summer! On the *Divina Costiera,* under that, that—angry old lion, the sun, and the—insincere sympathy of the— [*Her mood suddenly reverses again.*] No, no, no, I don't want her goddamn sympathy, I'll take that slobbery stuff off the tape and— *Begin! Continue! Dictation!* [*She rises, paces the forestage with a portable "mike."*]

[*A phrase of lyrical music is heard. She stops short, lifting a jeweled hand as if to say "Listen!" Then suddenly the accre-*

11

tion of years is broken through. The stage dims out except for her follow-spot on the forestage.]

"Cloudy symbols of a—high romance . . ." Who said that, where is that from? Check tomorrow, Blackie, in the *Book of Familiar Quotations* . . . Begin, continue dictation.

[*A pause, while she paces back and forth.*]

The love of true understanding isn't something a man brings up the road to you every day or once in a blue moon, even. But it was brought to me once, almost too late but not quite. . . .

The hard shell of my heart, the calcium deposits grown around it, could still be cracked, broken through, and my last husband broke through it, and I was brought back to life and almost back to—what?—Youth. . . .

The nights, the nights, especially the first one I spent with Alex! The way that a lover undresses, removes his clothes the first night you spend together, is a clue, a definite clue, to your whole future relationship with him, you know. Alex unclothed himself *unconsciously gracefully,* as if before no one in a—room made of windows, and then, unclothed—*correction:* clothed in a god's perfection, his naked body!—he went from window to window, all the way round the bedroom, drawing the curtains together so that daybreak beginning wouldn't wake us early from the sleep after love, which is a heavenly sleep that shouldn't be broken early. Then came to rest in a god's perfection beside me: reached up to turn off the light: I reached up and turned it *back on!*

[*At this point,* MRS. GOFORTH'S *watchdogs (lupos) set up a great clamor on the inland side of the mountain. A* MAN *shouts.* WOMAN SERVANTS *scream in Italian. Somebody calls, "Rudy, Rudy!"* MRS. GOFORTH *is very annoyed by this disruption of her tender recollections: she presses various buttons on the intercom box on her desk.*]

12

MRS. GOFORTH [*shouting over the dogs*]: *Che succede! Che fa, Cretini! Stronzi!* [*etc.*]

[*The savage barking continues but diminishes a little in volume as a* YOUNG MAN, *who has just been assaulted by dogs, limps and stumbles onto the terrace. He bears a heavy white sack over his shoulder, looking back as if to make sure he's no longer pursued.* BLACKIE *appears behind him, panting, looking as if she'd also been roughed up by the dogs.*]

BLACKIE [*to the* YOUNG MAN]: Places go mad, it's catching, people catch it! [*She draws a breath.*] There's a doctor up here, I'll get him for you.

CHRIS: Can I see Mrs. Goforth?

BLACKIE: Sit down somewhere. I'll see if she can see you, and I'll—

[*The* YOUNG MAN, CHRIS, *limps out upon the forestage, sinks onto a white iron bench. A wave crashes below the mountain. He looks blankly out at the audience for a moment, then shakes his head and utters a desperate-sounding laugh.* BLACKIE *rushes into the library area.*]

Mrs. Goforth, I can't stand this sort of thing!

MRS. GOFORTH: *What?*

BLACKIE: Those dogs of Rudy's, those wolves, attacked a young man just now.

MRS. GOFORTH: What young man, doing what?

BLACKIE: He was climbing the mountain to see you!

MRS. GOFORTH: Who is he, what does he want?

BLACKIE: I didn't stop to ask that. I had to drive the dogs off to keep him from being torn to pieces before I—asked him questions. Look! [*She shows* MRS. GOFORTH *a laceration on her*

13

thigh, just over the knee.] The others just watched and screamed like children at a circus!

MRS. GOFORTH: Sit down, have a brandy. A place like this is always protected by dogs.

[*There is the sound of another wave crashing.*]

CHRIS: Boom. [*He discovers that his leather pants, lederhosen, have been split down his thigh.*]

BLACKIE: That gangster's bodyguard, Rudy, just stood there and watched!

MRS. GOFORTH: Blackie, this estate contains things appraised by Lloyd's at over two million pounds sterling, besides my jewels and summer furs, and that's why it has to be guarded against trespassers, uninvited intruders. Have you had your anti-tetanus shot, or—whatever they call it?

BLACKIE: Yes, I'm all right but he isn't. [*She presses a button on the intercom box.*]

MRS. GOFORTH: Who're you calling?

BLACKIE: I'm calling Dr. Lullo.

MRS. GOFORTH: Stop that, leave that to me! Do you think I want to be sued by this trespasser? Get away from my desk. I'm going to buzz Rudy. [*She presses another button.*] Rudy, *dove* Rudy? *Io lo voglio in libreria, subito, presto! Capito?*

[*The* YOUNG MAN *staggers to his feet and calls:* "Mrs. Goforth!" MRS. GOFORTH *picks up a pair of binoculars and gazes out at the terrace.* BLACKIE *stares at her with consternation.*]

CHRIS: Mrs. Goforth?

[RUDY, *the watchman, in semi-military costume, appears on the terrace.*]

RUDY: Shut up, stop that shouting. [*He enters the library area.*]

MRS. GOFORTH: Aw. Rudy. What happened, what's the report?

RUDY: I caught this man out there climbing up here from the highway.

BLACKIE: He set the dogs on him.

MRS. GOFORTH: That's what the dogs are here for. Rudy, what's the sign say on the gate on the highway?

RUDY: "Private Property."

MRS. GOFORTH: Just "Private Property," not "Beware of Dogs"?

RUDY: There's nothing about dogs down there.

MRS. GOFORTH: Well, for Chrissake, put up "Beware of Dogs," too. Put it up right away. If this man sues me, I've got to prove *there was a "Beware of Dogs"* sign.

BLACKIE: How can you prove what's not true?

MRS. GOFORTH: [*To* RUDY]. Go on, hurry it up!

[*Rudy leaves.*]

MRS. GOFORTH [to BLACKIE]: Now pull yourself together. What a day! It's too much for me, I'll have to go back to bed. . . .

[GIULIO, the gardener's son, a boy of seventeen, appears on the terrace.]

GIULIO [to the YOUNG MAN, who is applying an antiseptic to his lacerations]: *Come va? Meglio?*

CHRIS: *Si, meglio, grazie.* Do you understand English?

15

GIULIO: Yes, English.

CHRIS: Good. Would you please tell Mrs. Goforth that Mr. Christopher Flanders is here to see her, and— Oh, give her this book, there's a letter in it, and—ask her if I may see her, don't—don't mention the dogs, just say I—I want very much to see her, if she's willing to see me. . . .

[*During this exchange on the forestage,* MRS. GOFORTH *has picked up a pair of binoculars.* GIULIO *knocks at the screen that represents the door between the terrace and the library.*]

MRS. GOFORTH: Come in, come in, *avanti!*

[*The* BOY *enters, excitedly.*]

GIULIO: Man bring this up road.

MRS. GOFORTH: [*gingerly accepting the book in her hand*]: Young man that dogs bite bring this—[*squints at book*]—to me?

GIULIO: This, this, brings! Up mountains!

[*She turns the book and squints at a photograph of the author.*]

MRS. GOFORTH: Man resemble this photo?

[BLACKIE *is still quietly weeping at the desk.*]

GIULIO: *Non capisco.*

MRS. GOFORTH: Man!—*Uomo!*—resemble, look like—this photo?

GIULIO: Yes, this man. This man that dogs bite on mountain. [*Points out excitedly toward the* YOUNG MAN *on the bench.*]

MRS. GOFORTH: Well, go back out—*vada fuori e dica*— Blackie! Tell him to go back out there and say that I am very upset over the accident with the dogs, but that I would like to know why he came here without invitation, and that I am not responsible for anybody that comes here without invitation!

16

BLACKIE: [*strongly, as she rises*]: No, I will not. I will not give a man nearly killed by dogs such an inhuman message.

MRS. GOFORTH: He hasn't been seriously hurt, he's standing up now. Listen he's shouting my name.

[*The* YOUNG MAN *has called, "Mrs. Goforth?" in a hoarse, panting voice. His shirt and one leg of his lederhosen have been nearly stripped off him. He has the opposite appearance to that which is ordinarily encountered in poets as they are popularly imagined. His appearance is rough and weathered; his eyes wild, haggard. He has the look of a powerful, battered, but still undefeated, fighter.*]

CHRIS: *Mrs. Goforth!*

[*His call is almost imperious. A wave crashes under the mountain:* CHRIS *closes his eyes, opens them, crosses to the lounge chair on the terrace and throws himself down in it, dropping a large canvas sack on the terrace tiles. The excited, distant barking of the dogs has now died out. Female voices are still heard exclaiming at a distance, in Italian.*]

MRS. GOFORTH: [*looking again through her binoculars*] Pull yourself together. The continent has been overrun by beatniks lately, I've been besieged by them, Blackie. Writers that don't write, painters that don't paint. A bunch of free-loaders, Blackie. They come over here on a Jugoslavian freighter with about a hundred dollars in travelers' checks and the summer addresses of everybody they think they can free-load on. That's why I'm not so sympathetic to them. Look, I made it, I got it because I made it, but they'll never work for a living as long as there is a name on their sucker list, Blackie. Now cut the hysterics now, and go out there and—

BLACKIE: *What?*

MRS. GOFORTH: Interrogate him for me!

17

BLACKIE: Interrogate? A badly injured young man?

MRS. GOFORTH: Trespasser! Get that straight in case he tries to sue me. [*She continues inspecting him through the binoculars.*] Hmm, he's not bad-looking, in a wild sort of way, but I'm afraid he's a beatnik. He has a beard and looks like he hasn't seen water for bathing purposes in a couple of weeks.

BLACKIE: You would, too, if a pack of wild dogs had attacked you.

MRS. GOFORTH: *Watchdogs, lupos,* defending private property: get that straight. He has on lederhosen. Hmm.— The first time I saw Alex, in the Bavarian Alps, he had on lederhosen and the right legs for 'em, too. And it's odd, it's a coincidence that I was dictating some recollections of Alex, who was a poet, when this young—*trespasser*—got here. Now if the sweat and the filthy appearance just come from the dogs' attack on him, I mean from *meeting* the dogs, you can tell by the smell of him while you're talking to him.

BLACKIE: You want me to go out and smell him? I'm not a dog, Mrs. Goforth.

MRS. GOFORTH: You don't have to be a dog to smell a beatnik. Sometimes they smell to high heaven because not washing is almost a religion with 'em. Why, last summer one of those ones you see in *Life* and *Look*, came up here. I had to talk to him with a handkerchief held to my nose. It was a short conversation and the last one between us.

[CHRIS *staggers up from the lounge chair and shouts:* "Mrs. Goforth."]

MRS. GOFORTH: What impudence, going on shouting at me like that!

BLACKIE: I think the least you could do is go out there your-

18

self and show some decent concern over the dogs' attack on him.

MRS. GOFORTH: I'm not going to see him till I've checked with my lawyers about my liability, if any. So be a good scout, a nice Brownie den-mother, and go out there and—

BLACKIE: *Interrogate* him?

MRS. GOFORTH: Ask him politely what he wants here, why he came to see me without invitation, and if you get the right answers, put him in the pink villino. And I'll see him later, after my siesta. He might be O.K. for a while, and I could use some male companionship up here since all I've got is you and Generalissimo Rudy for company this summer. I do need male company, Blackie, that's what I need to be me, the old Sissy Goforth, high, low, jack and the game!

BLACKIE: I'll go see if he's seriously hurt.

[*She crosses out, to the terrace, and approaches* CHRIS *limping about the forestage.*]

BLACKIE: [to CHRIS]. How are you, are you all right, now?

CHRIS: Not all right, but better. Could I see Mrs. Goforth?

BLACKIE: Not yet, not right now, but she told me to put you in the little pink guest house, if you can—walk a little. It's a little way down the mountain.

CHRIS: Well, thank God, and— [*He tries to lift his sack and stumbles under its weight.*] Mrs. Goforth, of course . . .

BLACKIE: [*calling*]: *Giulio! Vieni qui!*

[GIULIO *comes on to the terrace.*]

BLACKIE: *Porta questo sacco al villino rosa.*

GIULIO: [*lifting sack*]: *Pesante!—Dio* . . .

19

BLACKIE: *Tu sei pesante nella testa!* [*Then to* CHRIS] You can bathe and rest till Mrs. Goforth feels better and is ready to see you.

CHRIS: Oh.—Thanks . . .

[*He follows her off the terrace. The* STAGE ASSISTANTS *fold and remove the screen masking a bed upstage. The bed is small but rococo, and all pink. The* STAGE ASSISTANTS *return downstage with the screen and wait near* MRS. GOFORTH, *who is still watching the terrace scene through her binoculars.*]

MRS. GOFORTH: [*to herself*]: Ah, God . . . [*Raises a hand unconsciously to a pain in her chest.*]

[*The* STAGE ASSISTANTS *unfold the screen before her, as the library area is dimmed out.*]

SCENE TWO

The area representing the pink villino is lighted: the light is warm gold afternoon light and striated as if coming through half-open shutters. A cupid is lowered over the bed by a wire: there are smaller cupids on the four posts of the bed. BLACKIE, CHRIS, *and* GIULIO *enter the narrow lighted area, the young poet limping.* GIULIO *bears the canvas sack with difficulty, muttering* "Pesante!"

BLACKIE: Here you are, this is it. Now!

CHRIS: What?

BLACKIE: How are your legs? Mrs. Goforth keeps a doctor on the place, a resident physician, and I think he ought to come here and do a proper job on those dog-bites.

CHRIS: They're not that bad, really.

BLACKIE: Have you had shots?

CHRIS: Shots?

BLACKIE: For tetanus?

CHRIS: Yes, yes, sometime or other. I'm actually just—tired out.

BLACKIE: Giulio, see if the water's running in the bathroom. I'm sure you want to bathe before you rest, Mr. Flanders. Oh, oh, no covers on the bed.

CHRIS: Don't bother about covers on it.

BLACKIE: I think, I have an idea, you're going to sleep a good while, and you might as well sleep comfortably. Giulio. Covers for bed.

GIULIO: *Dove?*

BLACKIE: *Cerca nell' armadio del bagno.*

[GIULIO *goes out.* CHRIS *sits down on the foot of the narrow bed. His head falls forward.*]

Mr. Flanders! [*He pulls himself up.*] Please try to stay awake till the bed's made up and you've bathed.

CHRIS: Your name is—? [*He rises, unsteadily.*]

BLACKIE: Frances Black, called Blackie.

CHRIS: How do you do. Mine's Flanders, Christopher Flanders.

[GIULIO *enters.*]

GIULIO: *Non c'è acqua.*

BLACKIE: Well, tell your papa to turn the water on.

[GIULIO *tosses some pink silk sheets on the bed and runs back out.*]

I hope you don't mind camphor, the smell of camphor.

[*He shakes his head slightly, holding onto a bed post.*]

The water ought to be running in a minute.

CHRIS: I hope there's a shower. A tub wouldn't be safe for me. I don't think even drowning would wake me up.

BLACKIE: I'll wait here till you've bathed.

CHRIS: It's wonderful here after—yesterday in—Naples . . .

BLACKIE: Would you please get on the other side of the bed and help me spread these sheets?

[*He staggers around the bed. They make it up.*]

CHRIS: You—

BLACKIE: What?

CHRIS: I wondered if you're related to Mrs. Goforth or if you're—

BLACKIE: Not related. I'm working for Mrs. Goforth: secretarial work. She's writing a sort of—all right, you can sit down, now—she's writing her memoirs and I'm helping her with it, the little, as best I—can. . . .

[*He sinks back onto the bed and drops his head in his hands.*]

Mr. Flanders, the water's turned on, now.

CHRIS: [*staggering up*]: Oh. Good. Thank you. This way? [*Starts off.*]

BLACKIE: I'll fill the tub for you. Do you want warm or cold water, or—

CHRIS: Cold, please. Let me do it.

BLACKIE: No, just stay on your feet till it's ready for you.

[*She passes him and goes off. There is the sound of running water. He sits exhaustedly on the bed and sways. His forehead strikes the newel-post which is topped by a cupid. The room is full of painted and carved cupids. He looks up at the cupid on the post, shakes his head with a sad, wry grimace, drops his head in his hands, and slumps over again.*]

BLACKIE *returns from the bathroom with a towel-robe. She claps her hands.*]

BLACKIE: I told you to stay on your feet.

CHRIS: [*struggling up*]: Sorry. What is—I almost said "Where am I?"

BLACKIE: Here's a towel-robe for you. You'd better just duck in and out.

CHRIS: [*crossing to door and looking back at her from the threshold*]: Is this called the Cupid Room?

BLACKIE: I don't know if it's called that but it should be.

CHRIS: [*starting to leave but on threshold*]: What a remarkable bathtub, it's almost the size of a deck pool on a steamship.

BLACKIE: [*dryly*]: Yes, Mrs. Goforth thinks a bathtub should be built for at least two people.

CHRIS: [*entering*]: She must have been to Japan.

BLACKIE: Yes. She probably owns it.

[CHRIS *enters the bathroom: There is a splash, a loud gasp.*]

BLACKIE: Oh, I should have warned you, it's mountain spring water.

CHRIS: Does it come from a glacier?

[BLACKIE *picks up the cords of his rucksack to drag it away from the bedside. She finds it startlingly heavy. She kneels beside it to loosen the drawstrings, draws out a silvery section of some metalwork. She rises guiltily as CHRIS reappears in the towel-robe.*]

BLACKIE: You're—shivering.

CHRIS: For exercise. Shivering's good exercise.

24

BLACKIE: I don't think you need any more exercise for a while. How did you get this sack of yours up the mountain?

CHRIS: Carried it—from Genoa.

BLACKIE: I could hardly drag it away from the bed.

CHRIS: Yes, it's heavy with metal. I work in metal, now. I construct mobiles, but it's not the mobiles that are heavy, it's the metalsmith tools.

BLACKIE: You, uh—sell—mobiles, do you?

CHRIS: No, mostly give 'em away. Of course I—

BLACKIE: What?

CHRIS: Some things aren't made to be sold. Oh, you sell them, but they're not made for that, not for selling, they're made for—

BLACKIE: Making them?

CHRIS: Is there something buzzing in the room or is the buzz in my head? Oh, a wasp. It'll fly back out the shutter. Is this a cigarette box? [Opens box on small bedside table.] Empty.

BLACKIE: Have a Nazionale. [She offers him the pack.]

CHRIS: Thank you.

BLACKIE: I'll leave the pack here, I have more in my room.— Your hair's not dry, it's still wet. [He shakes his head like a spaniel.] Dry it with the towel and get right into bed. I have to get back to work now. I work here, I do secretarial work and I—

CHRIS: Don't go right away.

BLACKIE: You need to rest, right away.

CHRIS: The ice water woke me up.

BLACKIE: Just temporarily, maybe.

CHRIS: I'll rest much better if I know a bit more, such as—Did Mrs. Goforth remember who I was?

BLACKIE: I don't know about that but she liked your looks, if that's any comfort to you.

CHRIS: I didn't see her. She saw me?

BLACKIE: She inspected you through a pair of military field-glasses before she had me take you to the pink villa with the—king-size bathtub, the pink silk sheets, and the cupids.

CHRIS: Do they, uh—signify something?

BLACKIE: Everything signifies something. I'll—I'll shut the shutters and you get into bed. [*She turns away from him.*]

CHRIS: [*sitting on the bed*]: What is the program for me when I awake?

BLACKIE: [*with her back still toward him*]: Don't you make out your own programs?

CHRIS: Not when I'm visiting people. I try to adapt myself as well as I can to their programs, when I'm—visiting people.

BLACKIE: Is that much of the time?

CHRIS: Yes, that's—*most* of the time. . . .

BLACKIE: Well, I think you're in for a while, if you play your cards right. You do want to be in, don't you? After hauling that sack all the way from Genoa and up this mountain to Mrs. Goforth? Or have the pink silk sheets and the cupids scared you, worse than the dogs you ran into?

CHRIS: You have a sharp tongue, Blackie.

BLACKIE: I'm sorry but I was mistaken when I thought I had

26

strong nerves. They're finished for today if not for the season, for—years. . . . [*She starts away.*]

CHRIS: Have a cigarette with me. [*He extends the pack to her.*]

BLACKIE: You want to get some more information from me?

CHRIS: I'd sleep better if I knew a bit more.

BLACKIE: I wouldn't be too sure of *that.*

CHRIS: I've heard, I've been told, that Mrs. Goforth hasn't been well lately.

[BLACKIE *laughs as if startled.*]

CHRIS: She's lucky to have you with her.

BLACKIE: Why?

CHRIS: I can see you're—sympathetic and understanding about Mrs. Goforth's—condition, but—not sentimental about it. Aren't I right about that?

BLACKIE: I'm not understanding about it, and I'm afraid I've stopped being sympathetic. Mrs. Goforth is a dying monster. [*Rises.*] *Sorry, I'm talking too much!*

CHRIS: No, not enough. Go on.

BLACKIE: Why do you want to hear it?

CHRIS: I've climbed a mountain and fought off a wolf pack to see her.

BLACKIE: *Why?*

CHRIS: No where else to go, now.

BLACKIE: Well, that's an honest admission.

CHRIS: Let's stick to honest admissions.

27

BLACKIE: [*sitting back down by the bed*]: All right. I'll give you something to sleep on. You'll probably wish I hadn't but here it is. She eats nothing but pills: around the clock. And at night she has nightmares in spite of morphine injections. I rarely sleep a night through without an electric buzzer by my bed waking me up. I tried ignoring the buzzer, but found out that if I did she'd come stumbling out of her bedroom, onto the terrace, raving into a microphone that's connected to a tape-recorder, stumbling about and raving her—

CHRIS: Raving?

BLACKIE: Yes, her demented memoirs, her memories of her career as a great international beauty which she thinks she still is. I'm here, employed here, to—take down and type up these—

CHRIS: Memories?

BLACKIE: That's enough for you now. Don't you think so?

CHRIS: She doesn't know she's—

BLACKIE: Dying? Oh, no! Won't face it! Apparently never thought that her—legendary—existence—could go on less than forever! Insists she's only suffering from neuralgia, neuritis, allergies, and bursitis! Well? Can you still sleep? After this—bedtime story?

CHRIS: Blackie, I've had a good bit of experience with old dying ladies, scared to death of dying, ladies with lives like Mrs. Goforth's behind them, which they won't think are over, and I've discovered it's possible to give them, at least to offer them, something closer to what they need than what they think they still want. Yes. . . . Would you please throw me the strings of my sack, Blackie?

[*She tosses the strings to the bedside. He hauls the rucksack over, leans out of the bed to open it: removes a mobile.*]

28

Give her this for me, Blackie. It took me six months to make it. It has a name, a title. It's called "The Earth Is a Wheel in a Great Big Gambling Casino."

[*Music is heard playing softly.*]

BLACKIE:—"The Earth Is—"?

CHRIS: ". . . a Wheel in a Great Big Gambling Casino." I made it on hinges, it has to be unfolded before it's hung up. I think you'd better hang it up before you show it to her, if you don't mind, and in a place where it will turn in the wind, so it will make a—more impressive—impression. . . . And this is for you, this book. [*He hands a book to her.*]

BLACKIE: Poems?

CHRIS: It's a verse-adaptation I made of the writings of a Swami, a great Hindu teacher, my—teacher. Oh. One thing more. I'd like to make a phone call to a friend, an invalid lady, in Sicily—Taormina, a mountain above Taormina.— Would Mrs. Goforth object if I—?

BLACKIE: Not if she doesn't know. What's the number?

[*He gives her the number in Italian and is told that it will not go through for some time.*]

There'll be a delay. Is it very important?

CHRIS: Yes, it is. She's dying. Blackie? You're the kindest person I've met in a long, long time. . . .

BLACKIE [*Drawing a sheet over him*]: This sort of thing is just automatic in women.

CHRIS: Only in some of them, Blackie. [*His eyes fall shut.*]

BLACKIE: You're falling asleep.

CHRIS: Yes, automatic—like kindness in some women. . . . [*He *drops his cigarette and she picks it up and crosses to the phone.*]

BLACKIE: [*Into the phone*]: Mariella? Bring a tray of food up to the pink villa. Better make it cold things. The guest's asleep and won't wake up for hours. [*She hangs up, looks at* CHRIS *and exits with book.*]

[*Lights dim on this area and a spot of light immediately picks up* MRS. GOFORTH *on the terrace. The* STAGE ASSISTANTS *have set a screen before this area and light is brought up on the forestage which represents the terrace of the white villa. The* STAGE ASSISTANTS *remove a wide screen and we see* MRS. GOFORTH *with two servants,* GIULIO *and* SIMONETTA. MRS. GOFORTH *is preparing to take a sun bath on the terrace. Her appearance is bizarre. She has on a silk robe covered with the signs of the zodiac, and harlequin sunglasses with purple lenses.*]

MRS. GOFORTH [*in her very "pidgin" Italian*]: Table here. Capito? Tabolo. [*Points.*] Qui. On *tabolo*, I want— What are you grinning at?

GIULIO: [*very Neapolitan*]: *Niente, niente ma scusa!* [*He places table by chaise.*]

SIMONETTA: [*giggling*]: *Tabolo.*

MRS. GOFORTH: On *tabolo voglio—una bottiglia d'acqua minerale, San Pellegrino, capite, molto ghiacciata: capite?*

[SIMONETTA *giggles behind her hand at* GIULIO's *antic deference to the Signora.* MRS. GOFORTH *glares suspiciously from one to the other, turning from side to side like a bull wondering which way to charge.* BLACKIE *enters the terrace area with the mobile, folded.*]

Che stronzi! Both of 'em.

BLACKIE: You mustn't call them that, it has an insulting meaning.

MRS. GOFORTH: I know what it means and that's what I mean it to mean. Generalissimo Rudy says they sleep together and carry on together some nights right here on my terrace.

BLACKIE: They're from Naples, and—

MRS. GOFORTH: What's that got to do with it?

BLACKIE: —and Generalissimo Rudy wants the girl for himself, so he—

MRS. GOFORTH: *Will you please tell them what I want on the table by this chaise. Here?*

BLACKIE: What do you want on the table?

MRS. GOFORTH: I—want a cold bottle of *acqua minerale*, cigarettes, matches, my Bain-Soleil, my codeine and empirin tablets, a shot of cognac on the rocks, the Paris *Herald-Tribune*, the Rome *Daily American*, the Wall Street *Journal*, the London *Times* and *Express*, the— Hey, what did you do with the—

BLACKIE: The visitor?

MRS. GOFORTH: The beatnik trespasser, yes, and what the hell have you got there that rattles like a string of boxcars crossing a railyard switch?

BLACKIE: The young man's in the pink villa, where you told me to put him. This is something he gave me for me to give you. It seems he constructs mobiles.

MRS. GOFORTH: Mobiles? Constructs?

BLACKIE: Yes, those metal decorations. He gives them titles. This one's called "The Earth Is a Wheel in a Great Big Gambling Casino."

31

MRS. GOFORTH: Is it a present—or something he hopes he can sell me?

BLACKIE: It's a present. He wanted me to suspend it before you saw it, but since you've already seen it—shall I hang it up somewhere?

MRS. GOFORTH: No, just put it down somewhere and help me up. The sun is making me dizzy. I don't know why I came out here. What am I doing out here?

BLACKIE: I was going to remind you that Dr. Rengucci warned you not to expose yourself to the sun, till the chest abscess, the lesion, has healed completely.

MRS. GOFORTH: *I don't have a chest abscess!*— Stop putting bad mouth on me! Open the door, I'm going in the library. . . .

[*The* STAGE ASSISTANTS *rush out and remove the screen masking that area as* MRS. GOFORTH *starts toward it, lifting a hand like a Roman Empress saluting the populace.*]

MRS. GOFORTH: [*as she enters the library area*]: What did he have to say?

BLACKIE: The—?

MRS. GOFORTH: *Trespasser,* what did he have to say?

BLACKIE: About what?

MRS. GOFORTH: *Me.*

BLACKIE: He wondered if you remembered him or not.

MRS. GOFORTH: Oh, I might have met him somewhere, sometime or other, when I was still meeting people, interested in it, before they all seemed like the same person over and over and I got tired of the person.

32

BLACKIE: This young man won't seem like the same person to you.

MRS. GOFORTH: That remains to be— Blackie, y'know what I need to shake off this, this—depression, what would do me more good this summer than all the shots and pills in the pharmaceutical kingdom? I need me a lover.

BLACKIE: What do you mean by "a lover"?

MRS. GOFORTH: I mean a lover! What you *you* mean by a lover, or is that word outside your Vassar vocabulary?

BLACKIE: I've only had one lover, my husband Charles, and I lost Charles last spring.

MRS. GOFORTH: What beats me is how you could have a husband named Charles and not call him Charlie. I mean the fact that you called him Charles and not Charlie describes your whole relationship with him, don't it?

BLACKIE [*flaring*]: *Stop about my husband!*

MRS. GOFORTH: The dead are dead and the living are living!

BLACKIE: Not so, I'm not dead but not living!

MRS. GOFORTH: Giulio! [*He has entered the library area with the mineral water.*] *Va al villino rosa e portami qui* the sack— *il sacco!—dell' ospite là.*

BLACKIE: Oh, no, you mustn't do that, that's too undignified of you!

[GIULIO *goes out to perform this errand.*]

MRS. GOFORTH: Take care of your own dignity and lemme take care of mine. It's a perfectly natural, legitimate thing to do, to go through the luggage of a trespasser on your place for— possible—weapons, and so forth. . . . [*She sits at the desk.*] Pencil, notebook, dictation.

33

[BLACKIE *pays no attention to these demands, but lights a cigarette behind* MRS. GOFORTH'S *back as she begins dictating.*]

—Season of '24, costume ball at Cannes. Never mind the style, now. Polish up later. . . .

—Went as Lady Godiva. All of me, gilded, my whole body painted gold, except for—green velvet fig leaf. Breasts? Famous breats? Nude, nude completely!

—Astride a white horse, led into the ballroom by a young nigger. Correction. A Nubian—slave-boy. Appearance created a riot. Men clutched at my legs, trying to dismount me so they could *mount* me. Maddest party ever, ever imaginable in those days of mad parties. This set the record for madness. —In '29, so much ended, but not for me. I smelt the crash coming, animal instinct—very valuable asset. Put everything into absolutely indestructible utilities such as—Tel. and Tel., *electric power.* . . .

[GIULIO *enters with the rucksack.*]

GIULIO: *Ecco, il sacco!* [*Drops it before* MRS. GOFORTH *with a crash that makes her gasp.*]

BLACKIE: May I be excused? I don't want to take part in this.

MRS. GOFORTH: Stay here. You heard that noise, that wasn't just clothes, that was metal.

BLACKIE: Yes, I suppose he's come here to seize the mountain by force of arms.

MRS. GOFORTH [*to* GIULIO]: Giulio, open, *aprite!*

[GIULIO *opens the sack and the inspection begins.*]

BLACKIE: I told you he made mobiles. The sack's full of metalsmith's tools.

MRS. GOFORTH: He hauled this stuff up the mountain?

34

BLACKIE: It didn't fly up.

MRS. GOFORTH: He must have the back of a dray horse. Tell this idiot to hold the sack upside down and empty it all on the floor, he's taking things out like it was a Christmas stocking.

BLACKIE: I'll do it. He'd break everything. [*She carefully empties the contents of the sack onto the floor.*]

MRS. GOFORTH: See if he's got any travelers' checks and how much they amount to.

BLACKIE [*ignoring this order and picking up a book*]: He offered me this book, I forgot to take it.

MRS. GOFORTH [*glaring at the book through her glasses*]: *Meanings Known and Unknown*. It sounds like something religious.

BLACKIE: He says it's a verse-adaptation he did of a—

MRS. GOFORTH: Swami Something. See if you can locate the little book they always carry with names and addresses in it. Sometimes it gives you a clue to their backgrounds and—inclinations. Here. This is it. [*Snatches up an address book.*]— Christ, Lady Emerald Fowler, she's been in hell for ten years.— Christabel Smithers, that name rings a long-ago church bell for a dead bitch, too. Mary Cole, *dead!* Laurie Emerson, *dead!* Is he a graveyard sexton? My God, where's his passport?

BLACKIE [*picking it up*]: Here.

MRS. GOFORTH: Date of birth: 1928. Hmmm, no chicken, Blackie. How old's that make him?

BLACKIE: —Thirty-five.

[*She lights a cigarette.* MRS. GOFORTH *snatches the cigarette from* BLACKIE's *hand. She sets it on the desk and in a moment starts smoking it herself.*]

MRS. GOFORTH: No travelers' checks whatsoever. Did he have some cash on him?

BLACKIE: I don't know, I neglected to frisk him.

MRS. GOFORTH: Did you get him to bathe?

BLACKIE: Yes.

MRS. GOFORTH: How'd he look in the bathtub?

BLACKIE: I'm afraid I can't give you any report on that.

MRS. GOFORTH: Where's his clothes? No clothes, *niente vestiti in sacco?*

GIULIO [*produces one shirt, laundered but not ironed*]: *Ecco una camicia, una bella camicia!*

MRS. GOFORTH: One shirt!

BLACKIE: He probably had to check some of his luggage somewhere, in order to get up the—goatpath . . . and the clothes he had on were demolished by Rudy's dogs.

MRS. GOFORTH: Well, put a robe in his room. I know—the Samurai warrior's robe that Alex wore at breakfast. We always wore robes at breakfast in case we wanted to go back to bed right after. . . .

[A STAGE ASSISTANT *enters with an ancient Japanese robe, with a belt and sword attached.*]

BLACKIE: Did he keep the sword on him at breakfast?

MRS. GOFORTH: Yes, he did and sometimes he'd draw it out of the scabbard and poke me with it. Ho ho. Tickle me with the point of it, ho ho ho ho!

BLACKIE: You weren't afraid he'd—accidentally—?

MRS. GOFORTH: Sure, and it was exciting. I had me a little revolver. I'd draw a bead on him sometimes and I'd say, you

36

are too beautiful to live, and so you have to die, now, tonight—
tomorrow—

[*The* STAGE ASSISTANT *hands the robe to* BLACKIE, *who accepts it without a glance at him.*]

—put the robe in the pink villino, and then call the Witch of Capri.

BLACKIE: Which witch?

MRS. GOFORTH: The one that wired me last month: "Are you still living?" Tell her I am. And get her over for dinner, tell her it's *urgentissimo!* Everything's *urgentissimo* here this summer. . . .

[*Phone buzzes on desk. As* BLACKIE *starts off,* MRS. GOFORTH *answers the phone.*]

Pronto, pronto, chi parla?—Taormina? Sicilia?—I've placed no call to that place. [*She slams down the phone.*] —Hmmm, the summer is coming to life! I'm coming back to life with it!

[*She presses buttons on her intercom system. Electric buzzers sound from various points on the stage as the* STAGE ASSISTANTS *cover the library area with the griffin-crested screen.*]

THE SCENE DIMS OUT.

SCENE THREE

That evening. The setting is the terrace of the white villa and a small section of MRS. GOFORTH's *bedroom, upstage left. In this scene, the* STAGE ASSISTANTS *may double as* BUTLERS, *with or without white jackets. At the curtain's rise, the two screens are lighted, one masking the small dinner table on the forestage, the other* MRS. GOFORTH; *a* STAGE ASSISTANT *stands beside each screen so that they can be removed simultaneously when a chord provides the signal. The middle panel of* MRS. GOFORTH's *screen is topped by a gold-winged griffin to signify that she is "in residence" behind it.*

MRS. GOFORTH'S VOICE [*asthmatically*]: *Simonetta, la roba.*

[SIMONETTA *rushes behind the screen with an elaborate Oriental costume.*]

Attenzione, goddamn it, *questa roba molto, molto valore. Va bene. Adesso, parruca!**

SIMONETTA [*emerging from the screen*]: *A parruca bionda?*

MRS. GOFORTH: *Nera, nera!*

[*There is heard a reedy chord as on a harmonium. The screens are whisked away. In the stage-left area, we see* MRS. GOFORTH *in the Oriental robe, on the forestage,* RUDY *in his semi-military outfit pouring himself a drink, and a small section of balustrade on which is a copper brazier, flickering with blue flame.* BLACKIE *enters, stage right, with a napkin and silver and sets a third place at the table,* RUDY *hovers behind her.*]

BLACKIE: Stop breathing down my neck.

MRS. GOFORTH: *Ecco!*

[*She puts on a black Kabuki wig with fantastic ornaments*

---

* Wig.

stuck in it. Her appearance is gorgeously bizarre. As she moves, out upon the forestage, there is Oriental music.]

Well, no comment, Blackie?

BLACKIE: The Witch of Capri has just gotten out of the boat and is getting into the funicular.

MRS. GOFORTH: You kill me, Blackie, you do, you literally kill me. I come out here in this fantastic costume and all you say is the Witch of Capri has landed.

BLACKIE: I told you how fantastic it was when you wore it last week-end, when that Italian screen star didn't show up for dinner, so I didn't think it would be necessary to tell you again, but what I do want to tell you is that I wish you'd explain to Rudy that I find him resistible, and when I say resistible I'm putting it as politely as I know how.

MRS. GOFORTH: What's Rudy doing to you?

BLACKIE: Standing behind me, and—

MRS. GOFORTH: You want him in front of you, Blackie?

BLACKIE: I want him off the terrace while I'm on it.

MRS. GOFORTH: Rudy, you'd better go check my bedroom safe. These rocks I've put on tonight are so hot they're radioactive. [*to* BLACKIE] Guess what I'm worth on the hoof in this regalia?

BLACKIE: I'm no good at guessing the value of—

MRS. GOFORTH: I can't stand anything false. Even my kidney stones, if I had kidney stones, would be genuine diamonds fit for a Queen's crown, Blackie.

[BLACKIE *lights a cigarette.* MRS. GOFORTH *takes the cigarette from her.*]

A witch and a bitch always dress up for each other, because

39

otherwise the witch would upstage the bitch, or the bitch would upstage the witch, and the result would be havoc.

BLACKIE: Fine feathers flying in all directions?

MRS. GOFORTH: That's right. The Witch has a fairly large collection of rocks herself, but no important pieces. [*She crosses, smoking, to the table.*] Hey. The table's set for three. Are you having dinner with us?

BLACKIE: Not this evening, thanks, I have to catch up on my typing.

MRS. GOFORTH: Then who's this third place set for?

BLACKIE: The young man in the pink villa, I thought he'd be dining with you.

MRS. GOFORTH: That was presumptuous of you. He's having no meals with me till I know more about him. The Witch of Capri can give me the low-down on him. In fact, the only reason I asked the Witch to dinner was to get the low-down on this mountain climber.

THE WITCH [*at a distance*]: Yoo-hoo!

MRS. GOFORTH: Yooo-hooo! She won't be here more than a minute before she makes some disparaging comment on my appearance. Codeine, empirin, brandy, before she gets here. She takes a morbid interest in the health of her friends because her own's on the downgrade.

THE WITCH [*nearer*]: Yoo-hoo!

MRS. GOFORTH: Yooo-hooo! Here she comes, here comes the Witch.

[THE WITCH OF CAPRI, *the Marchesa Constance Ridgeway-Condotti, appears on the terrace. She looks like a creature out of a sophisticated fairy tale, her costume like something*

40

that might have been designed for Fata Morgana. Her dress is gray chiffon, paneled, and on her blue-tinted head she wears a cone-shaped hat studded with pearls, the peak of it draped with the material of her dress. Her expressive, claw-like hands are aglitter with gems. At the sight of MRS. GO-FORTH, *she halts dramatically, opening her eyes very wide for a moment, as if confronted by a frightening apparition, then she utters a dramatic little cry and extends her arms in a counterfeit gesture of pity.*]

THE WITCH: *Sissy! Love!*

MRS. GOFORTH: Connie . . .

[*They embrace ritually and coolly, then stand back from each other with sizing-up stares.*]

THE WITCH: Sissy, don't tell me we're having a Chinese dinner.

MRS. GOFORTH: This isn't a Chinese robe, it's a Kabuki dancer's, a Japanese national treasure that Simon Willingham bought me on our reconciliation trip to Japan. It's only some centuries old. I had to sneak it through customs—Japanese customs—by wearing it tucked up under a chinchilla coat. Y'know I studied Kabuki, and got to be very good at it. I was a guest artist once at a thing for typhoon relief, and I can still do it, you see.

[*She opens her lacquered fan and executes some Kabuki dance movements, humming weirdly. The effect has a sort of grotesque beauty, but she is suddenly dizzy and staggers against the table.* THE WITCH *utters a shrill cry;* BLACKIE *rushes to catch her and support the table.* MRS. GOFORTH *tries to laugh it off.*]

Ha, ha, too much codeine, I took a little codeine for my neuralgia before you got here.

THE WITCH: Well, I'm suffering, too. We're suffering together.

41

Will you look at my arm. [*She draws up her flowing sleeve to expose a bandaged forearm.*] The sea is full of Medusas.

MRS. GOFORTH: Full of what?

THE WITCH: Medusas, you know, those jellyfish that sting. The Latins call them Medusas, and one of them got me this morning, a giant one, at the *Piccola Marina*. I want a martini. . . . I've got to stay slightly drunk to bear the pain. [*She tosses her parasol to* BLACKIE *and advances to the liquor cart.*] Sissy, your view is a *meraviglia, veramente una meraviglia!* [*She drains a martini that* BLACKIE *pours her, then swings full circle and dizzily returns to a chair at the table.*] Do we have to eat?— I'm so full of canapés from Mona's cocktail do . . .

MRS. GOFORTH: Oh, is that what you're full of? We're having a very light supper, because the smell of food after codeine nauseates me, Connie.

BLACKIE: Mrs. Goforth, shouldn't I take something to your house guest since he's not dining with you?

MRS. GOFORTH: No, meaning no, but you can leave us now, Blackie. Oh, excuse me, this is my secretary, Miss Black. Blackie, this is—what's your latest name, Connie?

THE WITCH: I mailed you my wedding invitation the spring before last spring to some hospital in Boston, the Leahey Clinic, and never received a word of acknowledgment from you.

MRS. GOFORTH: Oh, weddings and funerals're things you show up at or you don't according to where you are and—

[*She rings bell for service: the* STAGE ASSISTANTS *appear with white towels over their forearms or colored mess-jackets. Note: Although they sometimes take part in the action of the play, the characters in the play never appear to notice the* STAGE ASSISTANTS.]

42

—*other* circumstances: Have a gull's egg, Connie.

THE WITCH: No, thank you, I can't stand gulls.

MRS. GOFORTH: Well, eating their eggs cuts down on their population.

THE WITCH: What is this monster of the deep?

MRS. GOFORTH: *Dentice, dentice freddo.*

THE WITCH: It has a horrid expression on its face.

MRS. GOFORTH: Don't look at it, just eat it.

THE WITCH: Couldn't possibly, thank you.

MRS. GOFORTH: Are you still living on blood transfusions, Connie? That's not good, it turns you into a vampire, a *pipistrella*, ha, ha. . . . Your neck's getting too thin, Connie. Is it true that you had that sheep embryo—plantation in—Switzerland? I heard so. I don't approve of it. It keys you up for a while and then you collapse, completely. The human system can't stand too much stimulation after—sixty. . . .

THE WITCH: What did they find out at the Leahey Clinic, Sissy?

MRS. GOFORTH: Oh, *that*, that was just a little—routine check-up. . . .

THE WITCH: When you called me today I was so relieved I could die: shouted "Hallelujah" silently, to myself. I'd heard such distressing rumors about you lately, Sissy.

MRS. GOFORTH: Rumors? Hell, what rumors?

THE WITCH [*crossing to the bar cart for a refill*]: I can't tell you the rumors that have been circulating about you since your house party last month. The ones you brought over from Capri came back to Capri with stories that I love you too much to repeat.

43

MRS. GOFORTH: Repeat them, Connie, repeat them.

THE WITCH: Are you sure you feel well enough to take them? [*She returns to her chair.*] Well—they said you were, well, that you seemed to be off your rocker. They said you spent the whole night shouting over loudspeakers so nobody could sleep, and that what you shouted was not to be *believed!*

MRS. GOFORTH: Oh, how *nice* of them, Connie. Capri's turned into a nest of vipers, Connie—and the sea is full of Medusas? Mmm. The Medusas are spawned by the bitches. You want to know the truth behind this gossip? Or would you rather believe a pack of malicious inventions?

THE WITCH: You know I love you, Sissy. What's the truth?

MRS. GOFORTH: Not that.—I'll tell you the truth. [*She rises and indicates the intercom speaker.*] I'm writing my memoirs this summer. I've got the whole place wired for sound, a sort of very elaborate intercom or walkie-talkie system, so I can dictate to my secretary, Blackie. I buzz my secretary any time of the day and night and continue dictating to her. That's the truth, the true story. [*She goes over to* THE WITCH.]

THE WITCH: [*taking her hand*]: I'm so glad you told me, Sissy, love!

MRS. GOFORTH: Has it ever struck you, Connie, that life is all memory, except for the one present moment that goes by you so quick you hardly catch it going? It's really all memory, Connie, except for each passing moment. What I just now said to you is a memory now—recollection. Uh-hummm . . . [*She paces the terrace.*] —I'm up now. When I was at the table is a memory, now. [*She arrives at the edge of lighted area downstage right, and turns.*] —when I turned at the other end of the terrace is a memory, now. . . .

[THE WITCH *gets up and goes toward her.*]

44

Practically everything is a memory to me, now, so I'm writing my memoirs. . . . [*She points up.*] Shooting star: it's shot:—a memory now. Four husbands, all memory now. All lovers, all memory now.

THE WITCH: So you're writing your memoirs.

MRS. GOFORTH: Devoting all of me to it, and all of my time. . . . At noon today, I was dictating to Blackie on a tape-recorder: the beautiful part of my life, my love with Alex, my final marriage. Alex . . .

THE WITCH: [*going to the bar cart*]: Oh, the young Russian dancer from the Diaghilev troupe?

MRS. GOFORTH [*returning to her chair*]: Oh, God, no, I never married a dancer. Slept with a couple but never married a one. They're too narcissistic for me; they love only mirrors. Nope, Alex was a young poet with a spirit that was as beautiful as his body, the only one I married that wasn't rich as Croesus. Alex made love without mirrors. He used my eyes for his mirrors. The only husband I've had, of the six I've had, that I could make love to with a bright light burning over the bed. Hundred-watt bulbs overhead! To see, while we loved. . . .

THE WITCH [*going back to the table with the pitcher of martinis*]: Are you dictating this. Over a loudspeaker?

MRS. GOFORTH: Ah, God—Alex . . .

THE WITCH: Are you in pain? Do you have a pain in your chest?

MRS. GOFORTH: Why?

THE WITCH: You keep touching your chest.

MRS. GOFORTH: Emotion. I've been very emotional all day. . . . At noon today, a young poet came up the goatpath from the

45

highway just as I was in the emotional—throes—of dictating my memories of young Alex. . . .

THE WITCH: [*draining her martini*]: Ah-ha.

MRS. GOFORTH: He came up the goatpath from the Amalfi Drive wearing lederhosen like Alex was wearing the first time I set eyes on him.

THE WITCH [*starting to pour another martini*]: Ahh-ha!

MRS. GOFORTH [*snatching the pitcher from* THE WITCH *and placing it on the floor*]: Do you want to hear this story?

THE WITCH: Liquor improves my concentration. Go on. You've met a new poet. What was the name of this poet?

MRS. GOFORTH: His name was on the book.

THE WITCH: Yes, sometimes they do put the author's name on a book.

MRS. GOFORTH [*unamused*]: Sanders? No. Manders? No.

THE WITCH: Flanders. Christopher Flanders. [*Makes large eyes.*] Is he still in circulation?

MRS. GOFORTH: I don't know if he's in circulation or not but I do know he came up here to see me and not by the boat and funicular, he—

THE WITCH [*moving toward* MRS. GOFORTH]: Well, God help you, Sissy.

MRS. GOFORTH: Why, is something wrong with him?

THE WITCH: Not if you're not superstitious. Are you superstitious?

MRS. GOFORTH: What's superstition got to do with—

THE WITCH: I've got to have a wee drop of brandy on this! [*She crosses over to the bar cart.*] This is really uncanny!

MRS. GOFORTH: *Well, come out with it, what?*

THE WITCH [*selecting the brandy bottle*]: I think I'd rather not tell you.

MRS. GOFORTH [*commandingly*]: *What?*

THE WITCH: Promise me not to be frightened?

MRS. GOFORTH: When've I ever been frightened? Of what? Not even that stiletto you've got for a tongue can scare me! [*She downs her own martini at a gulp.*] So what's the—

THE WITCH: Chris, poor Chris Flanders, he has the bad habit of coming to call on a lady just a step or two ahead of the undertaker. [*She sits down.*] Last summer, at Portofino, he stayed with some Texas oil people, and at supper one night that wicked old Duke of Parma, you know the one that we call the Parma Violet, he emptied a champagne bottle on Christopher's head and he said, "I christen thee, Christopher Flanders, the Angel of Death." The name has stuck to him, Sissy. Why, some people in our age bracket, we're senior citizens, Sissy, would set their dogs on him if he entered their grounds, but since you're not superstitious— Why isn't he dining here with us?

MRS. GOFORTH: I wanted some information about him before I—

THE WITCH: Let him stay here?

MRS. GOFORTH: He's here on probation. [*She rings for* GIULIO, *and then crosses center.*] I put him in the pink villa where he's been sleeping since noon, when he climbed up a goatpath to see me.

THE WITCH [*following* MRS. GOFORTH]: I hope he's not playing his sleeping trick on you, Sissy.

MRS. GOFORTH: Trick? Sleeping?

THE WITCH: Yes, last summer when he was with that Portofino

47

couple from Texas, they were thrown into panic when they heard his nickname, "Angel of Death," and told him that night to check out in the morning. Well, that night, he swallowed some sleeping pills that night, Sissy, but of course he took the precaution of leaving an early morning call so he could be found and revived before the pills could—

[MRS. GOFORTH *abruptly begins to leave.*]

Where're you going, Sissy?

MRS. GOFORTH: Follow me to the pink villa, hurry, hurry, I better make sure he's not playing that trick on me.

[*She rushes off.* THE WITCH *laughs wickedly as she follows. The* STAGE ASSISTANTS *immediately set a screen before this acting area and the light dims. Then they remove a screen upstage, and we see* CHRIS *asleep in the pink villa. A lullaby, perhaps the Brahms one is heard.* MRS. GOFORTH *and* THE WITCH *appear just on the edge of the small lighted area.*]

MRS. GOFORTH: Everything's pink in this villa, so it's called the pink villa.

THE WITCH: I see. That's logical, Sissy. Hmmm. There he is, sleeping.

MRS. GOFORTH [*in a shrill whisper as they draw closer to the bed*]: Can you tell if he's—?

[THE WITCH *removes her slippers, creeps to the bedside and touches his wrist.*]

—Well?

THE WITCH: Hush! [*She slips back to* MRS. GOFORTH.] You're lucky, Sissy. His pulse seems normal, he's sleeping normally, and he has a good color. [*She slips back to the bed, and bends her face to his.*] Let me see if there's liquor on his breath. No. It's sweet as a baby's.

48

MRS. GOFORTH: Don't go to bed with him!

THE WITCH: No, that's your privilege, Sissy.

MRS. GOFORTH [*moving downstage from the lighted area in a follow-spot*]: Come out here.

THE WITCH [*reluctantly following*]: You must have met him before.

MRS. GOFORTH: Oh, somewhere, sometime, when I was still meeting people, before they all seemed like the same person over and over, and I got tired of the—person.

THE WITCH: You know his story, don't you?

[*The* STAGE ASSISTANTS *place a section of balustrade, at an angle, beside them, and a copper brazier with the blue flame in it. The flame flickers eerily on* THE WITCH's *face as she tells what she knows of* CHRIS. *Music plays against her stylized recitation.*]

Sally Ferguson found him at a ski lodge in Nevada where he was working as a ski instructor.

MRS. GOFORTH: A poet, a ski instructor?

THE WITCH: Everything about him was like that, a contradiction. He taught Sally skiing at this Nevada lodge where Sally was trying to prove she was a generation younger than she was, and thought she could get away with it. Well, she should have stuck to the gentle slopes, since her bones had gone dry, but one day she took the ski lift to the top of the mountain, drank a hot buttered rum, and took off like a wild thing, a crazy bird, down the mountain, slammed into a tree, and broke her hip bone. Well, Christopher Flanders carried her back to the ski lodge. We all thought she was done for, but Chris worked a miracle on her that lasted for quite a while. He got her back on her pins after they'd pinned her broken hip together with steel pins.

49

They traveled together, to and from Europe together, but then one time in rough weather, on the promenade deck of one of the *Queen* ships, the *Mary*, he suddenly let go of her, she took a spill and her old hip bone broke again, too badly for steel pins to pin her back together again, and Sally gave up her travels except from one room to another, on a rolling couch pushed by Chris. We all advised her to let Chris go, like Chris had let go of her on the promenade deck of the *Mary*. Would She? Never! She called him "my saint," "my angel," till the day she died. And her children contested her will, so that Chris got nothing, just his poems published, dedicated to Sally. The book won a prize of some kind, and *Vogue* and *Harper's Bazaar* played it up big with lovely photos of Chris looking like what she called him, an angel, a saint. . . .

MRS. GOFORTH: Did he sleep with that old Ferguson bitch? Or was he just her Death Angel?

[*The phone rings on the bedside table: the area has remained softly lighted.* CHRIS *starts up, drops back, feigning sleep, as* MRS. GOFORTH *rushes to the phone and snatches it up.*

—*Pronto, dica.*— Taormina, Sicily? No, *sbagliato!*

[MRS. GOFORTH *looks with angry suspicion at* CHRIS, *who murmurs as if in sleep. She notices the food tray by the bed, and snatches it up, then returns to* THE WITCH, *downstage.*]

He's already making long-distance calls on the phone and look at this! He's had them bring him a food tray, and I am going to remove it, I can't stand guests, especially not invited, that act like they're in a hotel, charging calls and calling for room service. Come on, I'm turning out the lights.

THE WITCH: My slippers.

[*She slips back to the bed and picks up her slippers, lingering over* CHRIS. *Suddenly she bends to kiss him on the mouth. He*

50

rolls over quickly, shielding his lower face with an arm and uttering a grunt of distaste.

Possum!

[*The lights dim in the area, as* THE WITCH *moves downstage.* MRS. GOFORTH *has disappeared.*]

Siss? Sissy! Yoo-hoo!

MRS. GOFORTH [*from a distance*]: Yoo-hoo!

THE WITCH [*following*]: Yooooooooo-hoooooooooo . . .

[*The* STAGE ASSISTANTS *replace the screen that masked the pink villa bed. Then they fold and remove the screen before* BLACKIE'*s bed in the blue villa. The area remains dark until a faint dawn light appears on the cyclorama. Then* BLACKIE'*s bed is lighted, and we see her seated on it, brushing her dark hair with a silver-backed brush.*]

THE SCENE DIMS OUT.

SCENE FOUR

It is later that night. The terrace of the white villa. The Watch-man, RUDY, *sweeps the audience with the beam of his flashlight. We hear a long, anguished "Ahhhh" from behind the screen masking* MRS. GOFORTH's *bed.* RUDY, *as if he heard the outcry, turns the flashlight momentarily on the screen behind which it comes. He chuckles, sways drunkenly, then suddenly turns the light beam on* CHRIS *who has entered quietly from the wings, stage right.*

CHRIS [*shielding his eyes from the flashlight*]: Oh. Hello.

RUDY: You still prowling around here?

CHRIS [*agreeably*]: No, I'm—Well, yes, I'm— [*His smile fades as* RUDY *moves in closer.*] I just now woke up hungry. I didn't want to disturb anybody, so I—

RUDY: You just now woke up, huh?

CHRIS: Yes, I—

RUDY: Where'd you just now wake up?

CHRIS: In the, uh, guest house, the—

RUDY: Looking for the dogs again, are you? [*He whistles the dogs awake. They set up a clamor far away.*]

CHRIS: I told you I just now woke up hungry. I came out to see if—

RUDY: [*moving still closer and cutting in*]: Aw, you woke up *hungry?*

CHRIS: Yes. Famished.

RUDY: How about this, how'd you like to eat this, something like this, huh?

[*He thrusts his stick hard into* CHRIS's *stomach.* CHRIS *expells his breath in a "hah."*]

'Sthat feel good on your belly? Want some more of that, huh? huh?

[*He drives the stick again into* CHRIS's *stomach, so hard that* CHRIS *bends over, unable to speak.* BLACKIE *rushes onto the terrace in a dressing gown, her hair loose.*]

BLACKIE: *Rudy! What's going on here?*

[*The dogs, roused, are barking, still at a distance.*]

This young man is a guest of Mrs. Goforth. He's staying in the pink villa. Are you all right, Mr. Flanders?

[CHRIS *can't speak. He leans on a section of balustrade, bent over, making a retching sound.*]

Rudy, get off the terrace!—you drunk gorilla!

RUDY [*grinning*]: He's got the dry heaves, Blackie. He woke up hungry and he's got the dry heaves.

CHRIS: *Can't—catch—breath!*

[*From her bed behind the griffin-crested screen,* MRS. GOFORTH *cries out in her sleep, a long, anguished "Ahhhhh!" The dogs' barking subsides gradually. The "Ahhhhh" is repeated and a faint light appears behind her screen.* BLACKIE *turns on* RUDY, *fiercely.*]

BLACKIE: I said get off the terrace, now get off it.

RUDY: You shoulda told me you—

BLACKIE: Off it, off the terrace!

RUDY [*overlapping* BLACKIE's *speech*]: You got yourself a boy friend up here, Blackie! You should've let me know that.

BLACKIE: Mr. Flanders, I'll take you back to your place.

CHRIS [*gasping*]: Is there—anywhere closer—I could catch my breath?

[*She stands protectively near him as* RUDY *goes off the terrace, laughing.*

[*The* STAGE ASSISTANTS *rush out to remove a screen masking* BLACKIE'*s bed in the blue villa, indicating "Blackie's bedroom."* CHRIS *straightens slowly, still gasping. The* STAGE ASSISTANTS *leave. Then* CHRIS *and* BLACKIE *cross to her villino, represented only by a narrow blue-sheeted bed with a stand beside it that supports an intercom box.*]

BLACKIE: Now tell me just what happened so I can give a report to Mrs. Goforth tomorrow.

CHRIS: The truth is I was looking for something to eat. I've had no food for five days, Blackie, except some oranges that I picked on the road. And you know what the acid, the citric acid in oranges, does to an empty stomach, so I—I woke up feeling as if I had a—a bushel of burning sawdust in my stomach, and I—

BLACKIE: I had food sent to your room. You didn't find it?

CHRIS: No. God, no!

BLACKIE: Then the cook didn't send it, or it was taken out while you were sleeping, and I'm afraid you'll have to wait till morning for something to eat. You see, the only kitchen is in Mrs. Goforth's villa. It's locked up like a bank vault till Mrs. Goforth wakes up and has it opened.

CHRIS: How long is it till morning?

BLACKIE: Oh, my—watch has stopped. I'm a watch-winding person, but I forgot to wind it.

54

[*The sky has lightened a little and there is the sound of church bells at a distance.*]

CHRIS: The church-bells are waking up on the other mountains.

BLACKIE: Yes, it's, it must be near morning, but morning doesn't begin on Mrs. Goforth's mountain till she sleeps off her drugs and starts pressing buttons for the sun to come up. So—

CHRIS: What?

[*The intercom box comes alive with a shrill electric buzz.*]

BLACKIE: Oh, God, she's awake, buzzing for me!

CHRIS: Oh, then, could you ask her to open the kitchen? A glass of milk, just some milk, is all I—

BLACKIE: Mrs. Goforth isn't buzzing for morning, she's buzzing for me to take dictation and, oh, God, I don't think I can do it. I haven't slept tonight and I just couldn't take it right now, I—

CHRIS: Let me take it for you.

BLACKIE: No. I'll have to answer myself, or she'll come stumbling, raving out, and might fall off the cliff.

[*She presses a button on the intercom box.*]

Mrs. Goforth? Mrs. Goforth?

[*The* STAGE ASSISTANTS *remove the screen masking* MRS. GOFORTH's *bed, upstage left. We see her through the gauze curtains enclosing the bed. She pulls a cord, opening the curtains, and speaks hoarsely into a microphone.*]

MRS. GOFORTH: *Blackie? It's night, late night!*

BLACKIE: Yes, it's late, Mrs. Goforth.

MRS. GOFORTH: Don't answer: this is dictation. Don't interrupt me, this is clear as a vision. The death of Harlon Goforth, just

55

now—clearly—remembered, clear as a vision. It's night, late night, without sleep. He's crushing me under the awful weight of his body. Then suddenly he stops trying to make love to me. He says, "Flora, I have a pain in my head, a terrible pain in my head." And silently, to myself, I say, "Thank God," but out loud I say something else: "Tablets, you want your tablets?" He answers with the groan of—I reach up and turn on the light, and I see—death in his eyes! I see, I know. He has death in his eyes, and something worse in them, terror. I see terror in his eyes. I see it, I feel it, myself, and I get out of the bed, I get out of the bed as if escaping from quicksand! I don't look at him again, I move away from the bed. . . .

[*She rises from the bed, the microphone gripped in her hand.*

I move away from death, terror! I don't look back, I go straight to the door, the door onto the terrace!

[*She moves downstage with the microphone.*]

It's closed, I tear it open, I leave him alone with his death, his—

BLACKIE: She's out of bed, she's going out on the —

[*She rushes into the wings. The light dims on the blue villa bed.*]

MRS. GOFORTH [*dropping the microphone as she moves out on white villa terrace*]: I've gone out, now, I'm outside, I'm on the terrace, twenty-five stories over the high, high city of Goforth. I see lights blazing under the high, high terrace but not a light blazing as bright as the blaze of terror that I saw in his eyes!

[*She staggers to the edge of the forestage.*

Wind, cold wind, clean, clean! Release! Relief! Escape from—

[*She reaches the edges of the orchestra pit. A wave crashes loudly below.*]

56

I'm lost, blind, dying! I don't know where I—

BLACKIE [*rushing out behind her*]: Mrs. Goforth! Don't move! You're at the edge of the cliff!

MRS. GOFORTH [*stopping, her hands over her eyes*]: Blackie!

[*She sways.* BLACKIE *rushes forward to catch her.*] Blackie, don't leave me alone!

[*The stage is blacked out.*]

INTERMISSION.

SCENE FIVE

The scene is the terrace of the white villa the following morning.
MRS. GOFORTH *is standing on the terrace while dictating to*
BLACKIE, *who sits at a small table. Above the table and about the
balustrade are cascades of bougainvillaea. Coins of gold light,
reflected from the sea far below, flicker upon the playing area,
which is backed by fair sky. There has been a long, reflective
pause in the dictation.* MRS. GOFORTH *stands glaring somberly out
at the sea.*

MRS. GOFORTH: Blackie, I want to begin this chapter on a more
serious note.

[*She moves around to the right of the table. Then continues
emphatically and loudly.*]

Meaning of life!

BLACKIE: Dictation?

MRS. GOFORTH: Not yet, wait, don't rush me. [*Repeats in a
softer tone.*] Meaning of life . . .

[CHRIS *appears at the far end of the terrace. He wears the
Samurai robe.* BLACKIE *sees him, but* MRS. GOFORTH *doesn't.*
BLACKIE *indicates by gesture that he should not approach
yet.*]

Yes, I feel this chapter ought to begin with a serious comment
on the meaning of life, because y'know, sooner or later, a person's obliged to face it.

BLACKIE: Dictating now, Mrs. Goforth?

MRS. GOFORTH: No, no, thinking—reflecting, I'll raise my hand
when I begin the dictation. [*She raises a jeweled hand to demonstrate the signal that she will use.*]

BLACKIE: Begin now?

58

[CHRIS *smiles at her tone of voice.* BLACKIE *shrugs and closes her notebook, rises quietly, and goes up to* CHRIS, *who lights her cigarette.*]

MRS. GOFORTH: One time at Flora's Folly, which was the name of the sixteenth-century coach house, renovated, near Paris where I had my salon, my literary evenings, I brought up the question, "What is the meaning of life?" And do you know they treated it like a joke? Ha ha, very funny, Sissy can't be serious!— but she *was,* she *was.* . . .

CHRIS: I think she's started dictating. Is there something to eat?

BLACKIE: Black coffee and saccharine tablets.

CHRIS: That's *all?!*

BLACKIE: Soon as I get a chance, I'll raid the kitchen for you.

MRS. GOFORTH [*almost plaintively*]: Why is it considered ridiculous, bad taste, *mauvais gout,* to seriously consider and discuss the possible meaning of life, and only stylish to assume it's just—what?

[*The* STAGE ASSISTANTS *have come out of the wings.*]

ONE: Charade. Game.

TWO [*tossing a spangled ball to his partner*]: Pastime.

ONE [*tossing the ball back*]: Flora's Folly.

TWO [*tossing the ball back*]: Accident of atoms.

ONE [*returning ball*]: Resulting from indiscriminate copulation.

[BLACKIE *throws her cigarette away and returns to her former position. The* STAGE ASSISTANTS *withdraw.*]

59

MRS. GOFORTH: I've often wondered, but I've wondered *more* lately . . . meaning of *life*.

[*The* STAGE ASSISTANTS *reappear with a small table and two chairs. They wait in the wings for a moment before placing them. They then retire.*]

Sometimes I think, I suspect, that everything that we do is a way of—*not* thinking about it. Meaning of life, and meaning of death, too. . . . *What in hell are we doing?* [*She raises her jeweled hand.*] Just going from one goddamn frantic distraction to another, till finally one too many goddamn frantic distractions leads to disaster, and blackout? Eclipse of, total of sun?

[*She keeps staring out from the terrace, her head turning slowly right and left, into the swimming gold light below her, murmuring to herself, nodding a little, then shaking her head a little. Her small jeweled hands appear to be groping blindly for something. She coughs from time to time.*]

There's a fog coming in. See it over there, that fog coming in?

BLACKIE: No. It's perfectly clear in all directions this morning.

MRS. GOFORTH: When I woke up this morning, I said to my-self—

BLACKIE: Dictation?

MRS. GOFORTH: Shut up! I said to myself, "Oh, God, not morning again, oh, no, no, I can't bear it." But I *did*, I bore it. You really don't see that mist coming in out there?

BLACKIE [*closing her notebook*]: Mrs. Goforth, the young man in the pink villa, Mr. Flanders, is waiting out here to see you. He has on the Samurai robe you gave him to wear while his clothes are being repaired, and it's very becoming to him.

MRS. GOFORTH: Call him over.

BLACKIE: Mr. Flanders!

MRS. GOFORTH: Hey, Samurai! *Banzai!*

[*Approaching,* CHRIS *ducks under a brilliant cascade of bougainvillaea vine.*]

BLACKIE: You certainly had a long sleep.

CHRIS: Did I ever!

MRS. GOFORTH [*sitting*]: Did he ever, ho ho. He slept round the clock, but still has romantic shadows under his eyes! There was a chorus girl in the Follies—I used to be in the Follies, before my first marriage—when she'd show up with circles under her eyes, she'd say, "The blackbirds kissed me last night," meaning she's been too busy to sleep that night, ho ho. . . .

CHRIS: I was busy sleeping, just sleeping. [*He bends over her hand.*]

MRS. GOFORTH: No, no, none of that stuff. Old Georgia swamp-bitches don't go in for hand kissing but—*setzen Sie doon,* and— Are you coming out here for battle with that sword on?

CHRIS [*sitting*]: Oh. No, but—I ran into a pack of wild dogs on the mountain, yesterday, when I climbed up here.

MRS. GOFORTH: Yes, I heard about your little misunderstanding with the dogs. You don't seem much the worse for it. You're lucky they didn't get at— [*grins wickedly*] your *face.*

CHRIS: I'm sorry if it disturbed you, but their bite was worse than their bark.

MRS. GOFORTH: The Italians call them *lupos* which means wolves. These watchdogs, they're necessary for the protection of estates like this, but—didn't you notice the "Private Property" sign in English and Italian, and the "Beware of Dogs" sign when you started up that goatpath from the highway?

61

CHRIS: I don't think I noticed a reference to dogs, no. I don't remember any mention of dogs, in English or Italian.

BLACKIE [*quickly*]: Naturally not, the "Beware of Dogs" sign was put up *after* Mr. Flanders' "little misunderstanding with the dogs."

MRS. GOFORTH: Blackie, that is not so.

BLACKIE: Yes, it *is* so, I heard you ordering the sign put up after, just after the—

MRS. GOFORTH [*trembling with fury*]: Blackie! You have *work* to do, don't you?

BLACKIE: I've never taken a job that called for collusion in—falsehood!

MRS. GOFORTH [*mocking her*]: Oh, what virtue, what high moral character, Blackie.

CHRIS [*cutting in quickly*]: Mrs. Goforth, Miss Black, I obviously *did* enter and trespass on private property at my own risk.

MRS. GOFORTH: If that statement's typed up—Blackie, type it up—would you be willing to sign it, Mr. Flanders?

CHRIS: Certainly, yes, of course, but let me write it up in my own handwriting and sign it right now. I'd hate for you to think I'd—

BLACKIE: He was attacked again last night.

MRS. GOFORTH: Again, by dogs?

BLACKIE: Not by dogs, by a dog. Your watchman, Rudy, attacked him because he woke up hungry and came outside to—

MRS. GOFORTH [*rising*]: *Blackie, get off the terrace!*

BLACKIE: I want to get off this mountain gone mad with your

62

madness! I try to help you, I try to feel sorry for you because you're—

MRS. GOFORTH: What? What am I?

CHRIS: Please. [*He tears a page out of* BLACKIE'S *notebook and speaks to her quietly.*] It's all right. Go in.

MRS. GOFORTH: What did you say to that woman?

CHRIS: I said you're very upset, I said you're trembling.

MRS. GOFORTH: *I've been up here surrounded by traitors all summer!* [*She staggers.*] Ahhhhh!

[CHRIS *helps her into her chair.*]

God! God . . .

CHRIS: Now. [*He scribbles rapidly on the sheet of paper.*] Here. "I, Christopher Flanders, entered a gate marked 'Private' at my own risk and am solely responsible for a—misunderstanding with—dogs." Witnesses? Of the signature?

MRS. GOFORTH: Can you unscrew this bottle? [*She has been trying to open her codeine bottle.*]

CHRIS [*taking it from her and removing the cap*]: One?

MRS. GOFORTH: Two.— Thank you.— Brandy on that— [*She indicates liquor cart.*]

CHRIS: Courvoisier?

MRS. GOFORTH: Rémy-Martin.— Thank you.

CHRIS: Welcome. [*He resumes his seat and smiles at her warmly.*] Let me hold that glass for you.

[*She has spilled some of the brandy, her hand is shaking so violently.*]

MRS. GOFORTH: Thank you.— Ahh . . . [*She draws a deep*

breath, recovering herself.] You have nice teeth. Are they capped?

[CHRIS *shakes his head, smiling.*]

Well, you got beautiful teeth. In that respect nature's been favorable to you.

CHRIS: Thank you.

MRS. GOFORTH: Don't thank me, thank your dentist. [*She puts on lipstick, dabbing her nostrils with a bit of disposable tissue.*]

CHRIS: I've never been to a dentist—honestly not.

MRS. GOFORTH: Well, then, thank the Lord for the calcium that you got from your mother's milk. Well, I have a pretty wonderful set of teeth myself. In fact, my teeth are so good people think they are false. But look, look here! [*She takes her large incisors between thumb and forefinger to demonstrate the firmness of their attachment.*] See? Not even a bridge. In my whole mouth I've had exactly three fillings which are still there, put in there ten years ago! See them? [*She opens her mouth wide.*] This tooth here was slightly chipped when my daughter's third baby struck me in the mouth with the butt of a water pistol at Murray Bay. I told my daughter that girl would turn into a problem child, and it sure as hell did.— A little pocket-size bitch, getting bigger! I'm allergic to bitches. Although some people regard me as one myself . . . Sometimes *with* some justification. Want some coffee, Mr. Trojan Horse Guest?

CHRIS: Thanks, yes. Why do you call me that, a Trojan Horse Guest?

MRS. GOFORTH: Because you've arrived here without invitation, like the Trojan Horse got into Troy.

[*She rises shakily to pour him a cup of coffee from a silver urn on the smaller, upstage table. While her back is turned,*

CHRIS *quietly crumples the sheet from* BLACKIE's *notebook and throws it into the orchestra pit.*]

CHRIS: Don't you remember our meeting and conversation at the Ballet Ball, some years ago, quite a few, when you asked me to come here whenever I was in Europe?

MRS. GOFORTH: Passports expire and so do invitations. They've got to be renewed every couple of years.

CHRIS: Has my invitation expired?

MRS. GOFORTH: Coffee. We'll see about that, that remains to be seen. Don't you smoke with your coffee?

CHRIS: Usually, but I—

[*He indicates he has no cigarettes.* MRS. GOFORTH *smiles knowingly and opens a cigarette box on the table.*]

How does it feel, Mrs. Goforth, to be a legend in your own lifetime?

MRS. GOFORTH [*pleased*]: If that's a serious question, I'll give it a serious answer. A legend in my own lifetime, yes, I reckon I am. Well, I had certain advantages, endowments to start with: a face people naturally noticed and a figure that was not just sensational, but very durable, too. Some women my age, or younger, 've got breasts that look like a couple of mules hangin' their heads over the top rail of a fence. [*Touches her bosom.*] This is natural, not padded, not supported, and nothing's ever been lifted. Hell, I was born between a swamp and the wrong side of the tracks in One Street, Georgia, but not even that could stop me in my tracks, wrong side or right side, or no side. Hit show-biz at fifteen when a carnival show, I mean the manager of it, saw me and dug me on that *one street* in One Street, Georgia. I was billed at the Dixie Doxy, was just supposed to move my anatomy, but was smart enough to keep my tongue moving, too, and the verbal comments I made on my anatomical

65

motions while in motion were a public delight. So I breezed through show-biz like a tornado, rising from one-week "gigs" in the sticks to star billing in the Follies while still in m'teens, ho ho . . . and I was still in my teens when I married Harlon Goforth, a marriage into the Social Register and Dun and Brad-street's, both. Was barely out of my teens when I became his widow. Scared to make out a will, he died intestate, so every-thing went to me.

CHRIS: Marvelous. Amazing.

MRS. GOFORTH: That's right. All my life was and still is, except here, lately I'm a little run down, like a race horse that's been entered in just one race too many, even for me. . . . How do *you* feel about being a legend in your own lifetime? Huh?

CHRIS: Oh, *me!* I don't feel like a—mythological—griffin with gold wings, but this strong fresh wind's reviving me like I'd had a—terrific breakfast!

MRS. GOFORTH: Griffin, what's a griffin?

CHRIS: A force in life that's almost stronger than death. [*He springs up and turns to the booming sea.*] The sea's full of white race horses today. May I—would you mind if I—suggested a pro-gram for us? A picnic on the beach, rest on the rocks in the sun till nearly sundown, then we'd come back up here revitalized for whatever the lovely evening had to offer?

MRS. GOFORTH: What do you think it would have to offer?

CHRIS: Dinner on the terrace with the sea still booming? How is that for a program? Say, with music, a couple of tarantella dancers brought up from the village, and—

[RUDY *appears on the terrace.*]

RUDY: Mrs. Goforth, I've taken care of that for you. They're going—on the way out.

MRS. GOFORTH: No trouble?

RUDY: Oh, yeah, sure, they want to see the Signora.

MRS. GOFORTH: No, no, no. I won't see them!

[*But "they" are appearing upstage: the members of her kitchen staff, who have been discharged.*]

Here they come, hold them back!

[*She staggers up, turns her back on them. They cry out to her in Italian.* RUDY *rushes upstage and herds them violently off. A wave crashes.*]

CHRIS [*quietly*]: Boom. What was their—?

MRS. GOFORTH: What?

CHRIS: —transgression?

MRS. GOFORTH: They'd been robbing me blind. He caught them at it. We had—an inventory and discovered that—they'd been robbing me blind like I was—blind. . . .

CHRIS: [*his back to her, speaking as if to himself*]: When a wave breaks down there, it looks as delicate as a white lace fan, but I bet if it hit you, it would knock you against the rocks and break your bones. . . .

MRS. GOFORTH. What?

CHRIS: I said it's so wonderful here, after yesterday in Naples. . . .

MRS. GOFORTH: What was wrong with yesterday in Naples? Were you picked up for vagrancy in Naples?

CHRIS: I wasn't picked up for anything in Naples.

MRS. GOFORTH: That's worse than being picked up for vagrancy, baby.

[*She chuckles. He grins agreeably.*]

CHRIS: Mrs. Goforth, I'm going to tell you the truth.

MRS. GOFORTH: The truth is all you could tell me that I'd believe—so tell me the truth, Mr. Flanders.

CHRIS: I'll go back a little further than Naples, Mrs. Goforth. I'd drawn out all my savings to come over here this summer on a Jugoslavian freighter that landed at Genoa.

MRS. GOFORTH: You're leading up to financial troubles, aren't you?

CHRIS: Not so much that as—something harder, much harder, for me to deal with, a state of— Well, let me put it this way. Everybody has a sense of *reality* of some kind or other, some kind of sense of things being real or not real in his, his—particular —world. . . .

MRS. GOFORTH: I know what you mean. Go on.

CHRIS: I've lost it lately, this sense of reality in my particular world. We don't all live in the same world, you know, Mrs. Goforth. Oh, we all see the same things—sea, sun, sky, human faces and inhuman faces, but—they're different in *here!* [*Touches his forehead.*] And one person's sense of reality can be another person's sense of—well, of madness!—chaos!—and, and—

MRS. GOFORTH: Go on. I'm still with you.

CHRIS: And when one person's sense of reality, or loss of sense of reality, disturbs another one's sense of reality—I know how mixed up this—

MRS. GOFORTH: Not a bit, clear as a bell, so keep on, y'haven't lost my attention.

CHRIS: Being able to talk: wonderful! When one person's sense of reality seems too—disturbingly different from another person's, uh—

68

MRS. GOFORTH: Sense of reality. Continue.

CHRIS: Well, he's—avoided! Not welcome! It's—*that simple.*
. . . And—yesterday in Naples, I suddenly realized that I was
in that situation. [*He turns to the booming sea and says "Boom."*]
I found out that I was now a—*leper!*

MRS. GOFORTH: Leopard?

CHRIS: *Leper!*—Boom!

[*She ignores the "boom."*]

Yes, you see, they hang labels, tags of false identification on
people that disturb their own sense of reality too much, like
the bells that used to be hung on the necks of—lepers!—Boom!

The lady I'd come over to visit, who lives in a castle on the top
of Ravello, sent me a wire to Naples. I walked to Naples on foot
to pick it up, and picked it up at American Express in Naples,
and what it said was: "Not yet, not ready for you, dear—Angel
of—Death. . . ."

[*She regards him a bit uncomfortably. He smiles very warmly
at her; she relaxes.*]

MRS. GOFORTH: Ridiculous!

CHRIS: Yes, and inconvenient since I'd—

MRS. GOFORTH: Invested all your remaining capital in this standing invitation that had stopped standing, collapsed, ho, ho, ho!

CHRIS: —Yes . . .

MRS. GOFORTH: Who's this bitch at Ravello?

CHRIS: I'd rather forget her name, now.

MRS. GOFORTH: But you see you young people, well, you
reasonably young people who used to be younger, you get in
the habit of being sort of—professional house guests, and as you

69

get a bit older, and who doesn't get a bit older, some more than just a *bit* older, you're still professional house guests, and—

CHRIS: Yes?

MRS. GOFORTH: Oh, you have charm, all of you, you still have your good looks and charm and you all do something creative, such as writing but not writing, and painting but not painting, and that goes fine for a time but—

CHRIS: You've made your point, Mrs. Goforth.

MRS. GOFORTH. No, not yet, quite yet. Your case is special. You've gotten a special nickname, "dear Angel of Death." And it's lucky for you I couldn't be less superstitious, deliberately walk under ladders, think a black cat's as lucky as a white cat, am only against the human cats of this world, of which there's no small number. So! What're you looking around for, Angel of Death, as they call you?

CHRIS: I would love to have some buttered toast with my coffee.

MRS. GOFORTH: Oh, no toast with *my* coffee, buttered, un-buttered—no toast. For breakfast I have only black coffee. Anything solid takes the edge off my energy, and it's the time after breakfast when I do my best work.

CHRIS: What are you working on?

MRS. GOFORTH: My memories, my memoirs, night and day, to meet the publisher's deadlines. The pressure has brought on a sort of nervous breakdown, and I'm enjoying every minute of it because it has taken the form of making me absolutely frank and honest with people. No more pretenses, although I was always frank and honest with people, comparatively. But now much more so. No more pretenses at all . . .

CHRIS: It's wonderful.

70

MRS. GOFORTH. What?

CHRIS: That you and I have happened to meet at just this time, because I have reached the same point in my life as you say you have come to in yours.

MRS. GOFORTH [*suspiciously*]: What? Which? Point?

CHRIS: The point you mentioned, the point of no more pretenses.

MRS. GOFORTH: You say you've reached that point, too?

[CHRIS *nods, smiling warmly.*]

Hmmmm.

[*The sound is skeptical and so is the look she gives him.*]

CHRIS: It's *true*, I *have*, Mrs. Goforth.

MRS. GOFORTH: I don't mean to call you a liar or even a phantasist, but I don't see how you could afford to arrive at the point of no more pretenses, Chris.

CHRIS: I probably couldn't afford to arrive at that point any more than I could afford to travel this summer.

MRS. GOFORTH: Hmmm. I see. But you traveled?

CHRIS: Yes, mostly on foot, Mrs. Goforth—since—Genoa.

MRS. GOFORTH [*rising and walking near the balustrade*]: One of the reasons I took this place here is because it's supposed to be inaccessible except from the sea. Between here and the highway there's just a goatpath, hardly possible to get down, and I thought impossible to get up. Hmm. Yes. Well. But you got yourself up.

CHRIS [*pouring the last of the coffee*]: I had to. I had to get up it.

71

MRS. GOFORTH [*turning back to him and sitting*]: Let's play the truth game. Do you know the truth game?

CHRIS: Yes, but I don't like it. I've always made excuses to get out of it when it's played at parties because I think the truth is too delicate and, well, *dangerous* a thing to be played with at parties, Mrs. Goforth. It's nitroglycerin, it has to be handled with the—the carefulest care, or somebody hurts somebody and gets hurt back and the party turns to a—devastating explosion, people crying, people screaming, people even fighting and throwing things at each other. I've seen it happen, and there's no truth in it—that's true.

MRS. GOFORTH: But you say you've reached the same point that I have this summer, the point of no more pretenses, so why can't we play the truth game together, huh, Chris?

CHRIS: Why don't we put it off till—say, after—supper?

MRS. GOFORTH: You play it better on a full stomach, do you?

CHRIS: Yes, you have to be physically fortified for it as well as —morally fortified for it.

MRS. GOFORTH: And you'd like to stay for supper? You don't have any other engagement for supper?

CHRIS: I have no engagements of any kind now, Mrs. Goforth.

MRS. GOFORTH: Well, I don't know about supper. Sometimes I don't want any.

CHRIS: How about after—?

MRS. GOFORTH: —What?

CHRIS: After lunch?

MRS. GOFORTH: Oh, sometimes I don't have lunch, either.

CHRIS: You're not on a healthful regime. You know, the spirit

72

has to live in the body, and so you have to keep the body in a state of repair because it's the home of the—spirit. . . .

MRS. GOFORTH: Hmmm. Are you talking about your spirit and body, or mine?

CHRIS: Yours.

MRS. GOFORTH: One long-ago meeting between us, and you expect me to believe you care more about my spirit and body than your own, Mr. Flanders?

CHRIS: Mrs. Goforth, some people, some people, most of them, get panicky when they're not cared for by somebody, but I get panicky when I have no one to care for.

MRS. GOFORTH: Oh, you seem to be setting yourself up as a— as a saint of some kind. . . .

CHRIS: All I said is I need somebody to care for. I don't say that— [*He has finished his coffee and he crosses to the warmer for more.*] I'm playing the truth game with you. Caring for somebody gives me the sense of being—sheltered, protected. . . .

MRS. GOFORTH: "Sheltered, protected" from what?

CHRIS [*standing above her*]: Unreality!—lostness? Have you ever seen how two little animals sleep together, a pair of kittens or puppies? All day they seem so secure in the house of their master, but at night, when they sleep, they don't seem sure of their owner's true care for them. Then they draw close together, they curl up against each other, and now and then, if you watch them, you notice they nudge each other a little with their heads or their paws, exchange little signals between them. The signals mean: we're not in danger . . . sleep: we're close: it's safe here. Their owner's house is never a sure protection, a reliable shelter. Everything going on in it is mysterious to them, and no matter how hard they try to please, how do they know if they please? They hear so many sounds, voices, and see so many things they

73

can't comprehend! Oh, it's ever so much better than the petshop window, but what's become of their mother?—who warmed them and sheltered them and fed them until they were snatched away from her, for no reason they know. We're all of us living in a house we're not used to . . . a house full of—voices, noises, objects, strange shadows, light that's even stranger— We can't understand. We bark and jump around and try to—be—*pleasingly playful* in this big mysterious house but—in our hearts we're all very frightened of it. Don't you think so? Then it gets to be dark. We're left alone with each other. We have to creep close to each other and give those gentle little nudges with our paws and our muzzles before we can slip into—sleep and—rest for the next day's—playtime . . . and the next day's mysteries.

[*He lights a cigarette for her.* THE WITCH *enters dramatically on the terrace.*]

THE WITCH: The next day's mysteries! *Ecco, sono qui.*

MRS. GOFORTH [*with unconcealed displeasure*]: My Lord, are you still here?

THE WITCH [*as if amazed*]: Christopher! Flanders!

CHRIS: How do you do, Mrs.— Oh, I started to say Mrs. Ridgeway but that isn't it, now, is it?

THE WITCH: What a back number you are!

CHRIS [*drawing away from her*]: Yes.

MRS. GOFORTH: How'd you miss your return trip to Capri last night? I thought you'd gone back there last night. I had the boatman waiting up for you last night.

THE WITCH: Oh, last *night!* What confusion! [*She puts down her hat and follows* CHRIS.] When was the last time I saw you?

MRS. GOFORTH: If *you* don't know, why should he?

THE WITCH: Oh, at the wedding banquet those Texas oil people gave me in Portofino, oh, yes, you were staying with them, and so depressed over the loss of—

CHRIS [*cutting in*]: Yes. [*He moves toward the balustrade.*]

THE WITCH: You'd taken such beautiful care of that poor old ridiculous woman, but couldn't save her, and, oh, the old Duke of Parma did such a wicked thing to you, poured champagne on your head and—called you—what did he call you?

MRS. GOFORTH: Let him forget it, Connie.

[THE WITCH *gives her a glance and moves up to* CHRIS.]

THE WITCH: Something else awful happened and you were involved in some way but I can't remember the details.

CHRIS: Yes, it's better forgotten, Mrs. Goforth is right. Some of the details are much better forgotten if you'll let me—forget them. . . .

[MRS. GOFORTH *rises and starts to go inside.*]

THE WITCH: Are you leaving us, Sissy?

MRS. GOFORTH: I'm going to phone the boat house t'make sure there's a boat ready for your trip back to Capri, because I know you want back there as soon as possible, Connie. [*She goes into the library.*]

THE WITCH [*going to the table*]: Chris, you're not intending to *stay* here!?

CHRIS: Yes, if I'm invited: I would like to.

THE WITCH: Don't you know, can't you tell? Poor Sissy's going, she's gone. The shock I got last night when I—I had to drink myself blind!—when I saw her condition! [*She comes closer to him.*] You don't want to be stuck with a person in her appalling condition. You're young, have fun. Oh, Chris, you've been

75

foolish too long. The years you devoted to that old Ferguson bitch, and what did you get?

CHRIS [*lighting a cigarette*]: Get?

THE WITCH: Yes, get? She *had* you, you were *had!—left* you? *Nothing!*—I bet, or why would you be here?

CHRIS: Please don't make me be rude. We don't understand each other, which is natural, but don't make me say things to you that I don't want to say.

THE WITCH: What can you say to me that I haven't heard said?

CHRIS: Have you heard this said to your face about you: that you're the heart of a world that has no heart, the heartless world you live in—has anyone said that to you, Mrs. Ridgeway?

THE WITCH: Condotti, Marchesa Ridgeway-Condotti, Mr. Death Angel Flanders.

CHRIS: Yes, we both have new titles.

THE WITCH [*throwing back her head*]: Sally! Laurie! Sissy! It's time for death, old girls, beddy-bye! [*Less shrilly.*] Beddy-bye, old girls, the Death Angel's coming, no dreams . . .

CHRIS: I'm sorry you forced me to say what I feel about you.

THE WITCH: Oh, that. My heart pumps blood that isn't my own blood, it's the blood of anonymous blood donors. And as for the world I live in, you know it as well as I know it. Come to Capri, it's a mountain, too.

CHRIS [*moving away*]: You're not afraid of the nickname I've been given?

THE WITCH: No, I think it's a joke that you take seriously, Chris. You've gotten too solemn. [*She follows him.*] Let me take that curse off you. Come to Capri and I'll give you a party, decorated with your mobiles, and—

MRS. GOFORTH [*to* BLACKIE]: *See? She's out there putting the make on—*

[BLACKIE *leaves as* MRS. GOFORTH *comes from the library toward the terrace.*]

THE WITCH [*to* CHRIS]: You're pale, you look anemic, you look famished, you need someone to put you back in the picture, the social swim. Capri?

[MRS. GOFORTH, *on the terrace, advances behind* CHRIS *and* THE WITCH.]

MRS. GOFORTH: What picture? What swim? Capri?

THE WITCH: It's marvelous there this season.

MRS. GOFORTH: The sea is full of Medusas. Didn't you tell me the sea is full of Medusas, and a giant one got you?

THE WITCH [*crossing to her*]: Oh, they'll wash out, they'll be washed out by tomorrow.

MRS. GOFORTH: When are *you* going to wash out? I thought you'd washed out last night. I've ordered a boat to take you back to Capri.

THE WITCH: I can't go back to Capri in a dinner gown before sundown. [*She sits at the table and stares at* CHRIS.]

MRS. GOFORTH: Well, try my hot sulphur baths, or just look the place over, it's worth it. It's worth looking over. Me, I'm about to start work, so I can't talk to you right now. [*She gets* THE WITCH's *hat and brings it to her.*] I'm right on the edge of breaking through here today, I'm on a strict discipline, Connie, as I explained last night to you, and—[*She coughs, falls into her chair.*]

THE WITCH: Sissy, I don't like that cough.

MRS. GOFORTH: Hell, do you think I like it? Neuralgia, nerves, overwork, but I'm going to beat it, it isn't going to beat *me*, or it'll be the first thing that ever *did* beat me!

THE WITCH [*rising and going to her*]: Be brave, Sissy.

MRS. GOFORTH: Leave me alone, go, Connie, it'll do you in, too. [*She fumbles for a tissue.*]

THE WITCH [*looking wide-eyed at* CHRIS *and moving close to him*]: Watch out for each other!— Chris, give her the Swami's book you translated. *Ciao!* [*She throws him a kiss and moves off, calling back.*] *Questo è veramente una meraviglia . . . Ciao, arrivederci. . . . Amici!*

[THE WITCH *goes out of the lighted area and down the goat-path.* CHRIS *goes to the table and sits, looking about.*]

MRS. GOFORTH: What are you looking for now?

CHRIS: I was just looking for the cream and sugar.

MRS. GOFORTH: Never touch it. Y'want a saccharine tablet?

CHRIS: Oh, no, thanks, I—don't like the chemical taste.

MRS. GOFORTH [*coming to the table*]: Well, it's black coffee or else, I'm afraid, Mr. What?—Chris!

CHRIS: You have *three* villas here?

MRS. GOFORTH: One villa and two villinos. Villino means a small villa. I also have a little grass hut, very Polynesian—[*moving in front of the table*]—down on my private beach too. I have a special use for it, and a funny name for it, too.

CHRIS: Oh?

MRS. GOFORTH: Yes, I call it "the Oubliette." Ever heard of an oubliette?

CHRIS: A place where people are put to be forgotten?

MRS. GOFORTH: That's right, Chris. You've had some education along that line. [*She returns to where he sits.*]

CHRIS: Yes, quite a lot, Mrs. Goforth, especially lately.

MRS. GOFORTH: As for the use of it, well, I've been plagued by imposters lately, the last few summers. The continent has been overrun by imposters of celebrities, writers, actors, and so forth. I mean they arrive and say, like "I am Truman Capote." Well, they look a bit like him so you are taken in by the announcement, "I am Truman Capote," and you receive him cordially only to find out later it isn't the true Truman Capote, it's the false Truman Capote. Last summer I had the false Truman Capote, and the year before that I had the false Mary McCarthy. That's before I took to checking the passports of sudden visitors. Well—[*She moves to the opposite chair and sits facing him.*] as far as I know they're still down there in that little grass hut on the beach, where undesirables are transferred to, when the villas are overcrowded. The Oubliette. A medieval institution that I think, personally, was discarded too soon. It was a dungeon, where people were put for keeps to be forgotten. You say you know about it?

[CHRIS *stares straight at her, not answering by word or gesture. His look is gentle, troubled.*]

So that's what I call my little grass shack on the beach, I call it "the Oubliette" from the French verb "*oublier*" which means to forget, to forget, to put away and—

CHRIS: —forget. . . .

MRS. GOFORTH: And I do really forget 'em. Maybe you think I'm joking but it's the truth. Can't stand to be made a Patsy. Understand what I mean?

[*He nods.*]

This is nothing personal. You came with your book—[*picks up*

79

his book of poetry] with a photograph of you on it, which still looks like you just, well, ten years younger, but still unmistakably you. You're not the false Chris Flanders, I'm sure about that.

CHRIS: Thank you. I try not to be.

MRS. GOFORTH: However, I don't keep up with the new personalities in the world of art like I used to. Too much a waste of vital energy, Chris. Of course you're not exactly a new personality in it: would you say so?

[CHRIS *smiles and shakes his head slightly.*]

You're almost a veteran in it. I said a veteran, I didn't say a "has been—[*She sneezes violently.*] I'm allergic to something around here. I haven't found out just what, but when I do, oh, brother, watch it go!

CHRIS [*rising and bringing her a clean tissue*]: I hope it isn't the bougainvillaea vines.

MRS. GOFORTH: No, it isn't the bougainvillaea, but I'm having an allergy specialist flown down here from Rome to check me with every goddamn plant and animal on the place, and whatever it is has to go.

CHRIS: Have you tried breathing sea water?

MRS. GOFORTH: Oh, you want to drown me?

CHRIS [*returning to his chair and sitting*]: Ha ha, no. I meant have you tried snuffing it up in your nostrils to irrigate your nasal passages, Mrs. Goforth, it's sometimes a very effective treatment for—

MRS. GOFORTH: Aside from this allergy and a little neuralgia, sometimes more than a little, I'm a healthy woman. Know how I've kept in shape, my body, the way it still is?

80

CHRIS: Exercise?

MRS. GOFORTH: Yes! In bed! Plenty of it, still going on! . . . But there's this worship of youth in the States, this Whistler's Mother complex, you know what I mean, this idea that at a certain age a woman ought to resign herself to being a sweet old thing in a rocker. Well, last week-end, a man, a *young* man, came in my bedroom and it wasn't too easy to get him out of it. I had to be very firm about it.

[BLACKIE *appears on the terrace with a plate of food for* CHRIS. MRS. GOFORTH *rises.*]

What've you got there, Blackie?

BLACKIE: Mr. Flanders' breakfast. I'm sure he would like some.

MRS. GOFORTH: Aw, now, isn't that thoughtful. Put it down there.

[*As* BLACKIE *starts to put it down on the table,* MRS. GOFORTH *indicates the serving table.*

I said down there. And get me my menthol inhaler and Kleenex. I have run out.

[BLACKIE *sets the plate on the serving table and retires from the lighted area.*

Simonetta!

[MRS. GOFORTH *rings and hands the tray to* SIMONETTA *as she enters.*]

Take this away. I can't stand the smell of food now.

[SIMONETTA *goes out.*]

CHRIS [*who has moved toward the serving table and stands stunned*]: Mrs. Goforth, I feel that I have, I must have disturbed you, annoyed you—disturbed you because I—[*He crosses back to the table.*]

MRS. GOFORTH: Don't reach for a cigarette till I offer you one.

CHRIS: May I have one, Mrs. Goforth?

MRS. GOFORTH: Take one. Be my Trojan Horse Guest. Wait.

[*She moves beside him.*]

Kiss me for it.

[CHRIS *doesn't move.*]

Kiss me for it, I told you.

CHRIS [*putting the cigarette away*]: Mrs. Goforth, there are moments for kisses and moments not for kisses.

MRS. GOFORTH: This is a "not for kiss" moment?

[*He turns away, and she follows and takes his arm.*]

I've shocked *you* by my ferocity, have I? Sometimes I shock myself by it.

[*They move together toward the balustrade.*]

Look: a coin has two sides. On one side is an eagle, but on the other side is—something else. . . .

CHRIS: Yes, something else, usually some elderly potentate's profile.

[*She laughs appreciatively at his riposte and touches his shoulder. He moves a step away from her.*]

MRS. GOFORTH: Why didn't you grab the plate and run off with it?

CHRIS: Like a dog grabs a bone?

MRS. GOFORTH: Sure! Why not? It might've pleased me to see you show some fight.

CHRIS: I can fight if I have to, but the fighting style of dogs is not my style.

MRS. GOFORTH: *Grab, fight, or go hungry!* Nothing else works.

CHRIS: How is it possible for a woman of your reputation as a patron of arts and artists, to live up here, with all this beauty about you, and yet be—

MRS. GOFORTH: A bitch, a swamp-bitch, a devil? Oh, I see it, the view, but it makes me feel ugly this summer for some reason or other—bitchy, a female devil.

CHRIS: You'd like the view to be ugly to make you feel superior to it?

MRS. GOFORTH: [*turning to him*]: Why don't we sing that old church hymn:
"From Greenland's icy mountains to India's coral Isle
  Everything is beautiful . . ."

CHRIS: "Man alone is vile."

MRS. GOFORTH: Hmm. Devils can be driven out of the heart by the touch of a hand on a hand, or a mouth on a mouth. Because, like Alex said once, "Evil isn't a person: evil is a thing that comes sneaky-snaking into the heart of a person, and takes it over: a mean intruder, a *squatter!*"

CHRIS: May I touch your hand, please?

MRS. GOFORTH: [*as he does*]: Your hand's turned cold. I've shocked the warm blood out of it. Let me rub it back in.

CHRIS: Your hand's cold, too, Mrs. Goforth.

MRS. GOFORTH: Oh, that's just—nervous tension, never mind

83

that. I'll tell you something, Chris, you came here at a time unusually favorable to you. Now we're going to talk turkey. At least *I'm* going to talk turkey. You can talk ducks and geese, but I am going to talk turkey, cold turkey. You've come here at a time when I'm restless, bored, and shocked by the news of deaths of three friends in the States, one, two, three, like fire-crackers going off, right together almost, like rat-a-tat-tat blindfolded against the wall.— Well, you see I— [*She moves down to the lower terrace.*] I had a bad scare last winter. I was visiting relatives I'd set up on a grand estate on Long Island when some little psychosomatic symptom gave me a scare. They made a big deal of it, had me removed by a seaplane to the East River where they had an ambulance waiting for me, and whisked me off to a— Know what I said when I was advised to go under the knife the next day? Ha, I'll tell you, ha ha!— Called my law firm and dictated a letter cutting them off with one dollar apiece in my will. . . .

CHRIS [*who has come down to her*]: Mrs. Goforth, are you still afraid of— [*He hesitates.*]

MRS. GOFORTH: Death—never even think of it. [*She takes his arm and they move down to a bench, and sit.*]

CHRIS: Death is one moment, and life is so many of them.

MRS. GOFORTH: A million billion of them, if you think in terms of a lifetime as rich as mine's been, Chris.

CHRIS: Yes, life is something, death's nothing. . . .

MRS. GOFORTH: Nothing, nothing, but nothing. I've had to refer to many deaths in my memoirs. Oh, I don't think I'm immortal—I still go to sleep every night wondering if I'll—wake up the next day . . . [*Coughs and gasps for breath.*] —face that angry old lion.

CHRIS: Angry old—?

84

MRS. GOFORTH: —lion!

CHRIS: The sun? You think it's angry?

MRS. GOFORTH: Naturally, of course—looking down on—? Well, you know what it look down on. . . .

CHRIS: It seems to accept and understand things today. . . .

MRS. GOFORTH: It's just a big fire-ball that toughens the skin, including the skin of the heart.

CHRIS: How lovely the evenings must be here—when the fishing boats go out on the Gulf of Salerno with their little lamps shining.

MRS. GOFORTH: Well, they call this coast the *Divina Costiera*. That means the divine coast, you know.

CHRIS: Yes, I know. I suppose . . .

MRS. GOFORTH: You suppose what?

CHRIS: I suppose you dine on the terrace about the time the fishing boats go out with their little lamps and the stars come out of the—

MRS. GOFORTH: Firmament. Call it the firmament, not the sky, it's much more classy to call it the firmament, baby. How about spring? You write about spring and live in it, you write about love in the spring, haven't you written love-poems for susceptible—patrons?— Well! How many books of poems have you come out with?

CHRIS: Just the one that I brought you.

MRS. GOFORTH: You mean you burnt out as a poet?

CHRIS: —Pardon?

MRS. GOFORTH: You mean you burnt out as a poet?

85

[CHRIS *laughs uncomfortably.*]

Why're you laughing? I didn't say anything funny.

CHRIS: I didn't know I was laughing. Excuse me, Mrs. Goforth. But you are very—direct.

MRS. GOFORTH: Is that shocking?

CHRIS: No. No, not really. In fact I like that about you.

MRS. GOFORTH: But you give that little embarrassed laugh, like I'd made you uncomfortable.

CHRIS: My nerves are—

MRS. GOFORTH: Gone through like your list of suckers.[MRS. GOFORTH *sneezes and gets up to look for another tissue.*]

CHRIS [*standing*]: Mrs. Goforth—if you want me to go—

MRS. GOFORTH: That depends.

CHRIS: What does it depend on?

MRS. GOFORTH: Frankly, I'm very lonely up here this summer.

CHRIS: I can understand that.

MRS. GOFORTH: Now, you're not stupid. You're attractive to me. You know that you are. You've deliberately set out to be attractive to me, and you are. So don't be a free-loader.

[CHRIS *doesn't speak for a moment.*]

CHRIS [*gently*]: Mrs. Goforth, I think you've been exposed to the wrong kind of people and—

MRS. GOFORTH [*cutting in*]: I'm sick of moral blackmail! You know what that is. People imposing on you by the old, old trick of making you feel it would be unkind of you not to permit them to do it. In their hearts they despise you. So much they can't quite hide it. It pops out in sudden little remarks

86

and looks they give you. Busting with malice—because you have what they haven't. You know what some writer called that? "A robust conscience, and the Viking spirit in life!"

CHRIS [*going back on the terrace*]: Oh? Is that what he called it?

MRS. GOFORTH [*following*]: He called it that, and I have it! I give away nothing, I sell and I buy in my life, and I've always wound up with a profit, one way or another. You came up that hill from the highway with an old book of poems that you got published ten years ago, by playing on the terrible, desperate loneliness of a rich old broken-hipped woman, who, all she could do, was pretend that someone still loved her. . . .

CHRIS: You're talking about Mrs. Ferguson.

MRS. GOFORTH: Yes, I am.

CHRIS [*moving away from her*]: I made her walk again. She published my poems.

MRS. GOFORTH: How long after she published your poems did you let go of her arm so she fell on the deck of a steamship and her hip broke again?

CHRIS: I didn't let her go. She broke away from me—

[MRS. GOFORTH *laughs uproariously*]

—if you'll allow me to make a minor correction in the story. We were walking very slowly about the promenade deck of the *Queen Mary*, eight summers ago, more than a year after my poems were published. A young man called to her from a deck chair that we'd just passed, and she wheeled around and broke away from my hand, and slipped and fell, and her hip was broken again. Of course some malicious "friends" blamed me, but—I wouldn't leave her.

MRS. GOFORTH: No? She was still your meal-ticket?

87

CHRIS: Not at all.

MRS. GOFORTH: Who *was?*

CHRIS [*sitting*]: I was fashionable, then.

MRS. GOFORTH: Do you sit down while a lady is standing?

CHRIS [*springing up with a rather ferocious smile*]: Sorry, won't you sit down!

[*His tone is so commanding, abruptly, that she does sit down in the chair he jerks out for her.*]

May I tell you something about yourself? It may seem presumptuous of me to tell you this, but I'm going to tell you this: you're suffering more than you need to.

MRS. GOFORTH: I am—

CHRIS [*cutting through her protest*]: You're suffering from the worst of all human maladies, of all afflictions, and I don't mean one of the body, I mean the thing people feel when they go from room to room for no reason, and then they go back from room to room for no reason, and then they go *out* for no reason and come back *in* for no reason—

MRS. GOFORTH: You mean I'm alone here, don't you?

[CHRIS *takes hold of her hand. She snatches it away from him.*]

I'm *working* up here this summer, *working! Ever heard of it?*

[*A* STAGE ASSISTANT *appears in the wings as if she had shouted for him. He hands her a letter.*]

This morning's mail brought me this! My London publisher's letter! "Darling Flora: Your book of memoirs, *Facts and a Figure,* will, in my opinion, rank with and possibly—"

[*She squints, unable to decipher the letter further.* CHRIS *re-*

88

moves it from her trembling, jeweled hand, and completes the reading.]

CHRIS: "—rank with and possibly even out-rank the great Marcel Proust's *Remembrance of Things Past* as a social documentation of two continents in three decades. . . ."

MRS. GOFORTH: Well?

CHRIS: A letter like this should fall on a higher mountain.

MRS. GOFORTH: Huh?

CHRIS: A letter like this should be delivered above the snow line of an Alpine peak because it's snow, a snow job.

[*She snatches it back from him.*]

MRS. GOFORTH [*raging*]: For you, a blond beatnik, coming from Naples on foot up a goddamn goatpath, wearing at this table a Japanese robe because dogs tore your britches, I think your presumption is not excusable, Mister! It lacks the excuse of much youth, you're not young enough for your moxey. This publisher's not a lover. A lover might snow me, but this man's a business associate, and they don't snow you, not *me*, not *Sissy Goforth!* They don't snow me—*snow me!* They don't get up that early in the morning—

[*Her agitation somehow touches him. His smile turns warm again.*]

—that they could— [*coughs*] snow me. . . .

[*The* STAGE ASSISTANTS *lean, whispering together, as they retire from the stage.*]

CHRIS: Of course, without having your publisher's advantage of knowing *Facts and a Figure—*

MRS. GOFORTH: Nothing, not a word of it!

89

CHRIS: No, not a word, but what I was going to say was that I think you need *companionship*, not just employees about you, up here, but— How often do you see old friends or new friends this summer, Mrs. Goforth? Often or not so often?

MRS. GOFORTH: Hell, all I have to do is pick up a phone to crowd this mountain with—

CHRIS: Crowds? Is it that easy this summer? You're proud. You don't want to ask people up here that might not come, because they're pleasure-seekers, frantic choosers of silly little distractions, and—and—

MRS. GOFORTH: "and—and" *what?*

CHRIS: Your condition, the terrible strain of your work, makes you seem—eccentric, disturbing!— To those sea-level, those lower-than-sea-level, people. . . .

MRS. GOFORTH: *Get to whatever you're leading up to, will you!*

CHRIS: I notice you have trouble reading. I've been told I have a good reading voice.

MRS. GOFORTH: Most human voices are very monotonous to me. Besides, I'm more interested in producing literature this summer than having it read to me.

CHRIS: Mmm—but you do need some agreeable companionship.

MRS. GOFORTH: Right you are about *that*, but how do I know your idea of agreeable companionship is the same as mine? You purr at me like a cat, now, but a cat will purr at you one minute and scratch your eyes out the next.

[*He leans back, smiling, working the sword up and down in its scabbard.*]

I think you better take off that old sword belt.

90

CHRIS: There're no buttons on the robe, so without the belt on it—

MRS. GOFORTH: Take it off you!

CHRIS: The *robe?*

MRS. GOFORTH: The *sword* belt. You grin and fiddle with the hilt—the sword—like you had—evil—intentions.

CHRIS: Oh. You suspect I'm a possible assassin?

MRS. GOFORTH: *Take it off, give it here!*

CHRIS: All right. Formal surrender, *unconditional . . . nearly.* [*He takes the sword belt off and hands it to her.*]

MRS. GOFORTH: *O.K., Robert E. Lee! At Appomattox . . .*

[*She hurls the sword belt to the terrace tiles behind her. A* STAGE ASSISTANT *darts out of the wings to remove it. The other* ASSISTANT *laughs off stage.*]

CHRIS: Now what can I use for a sash to keep things proper?

MRS. GOFORTH: See if this goes around you, if being proper's so important to you.

[*She hands him a brilliant scarf she has been wearing about her throat. He turns upstage to tie the scarf about him. A phone is heard ringing, off stage.* BLACKIE *appears from behind the library screen.*]

MRS. GOFORTH [*to* BLACKIE]: Who's calling? My broker again, with the closing quotations?

BLACKIE: The call's for *Mr. Flanders.*

CHRIS: *Me,* for *me?* But who could know I'm up here!

MRS. GOFORTH: Cut the bull. You got a call up here last night. Business is picking up for you.

CHRIS: This is—mystifying!

BLACKIE: The phone's in the library.

CHRIS: Excuse me.

[*He goes quickly behind the library screen.* MRS. GOFORTH *crosses toward it but remains, listening, outside it.*]

CHRIS [*behind screen*]: *Pronto, pronto.* Madelyn!— How are you, how's your dear mother?— Oh, my God!— I meant to come straight down there but—was it, uh, what they call peaceful? [*Pause.*] Oh, I'm so glad, I prayed so hard that it *would* be! And I'm so relieved that it *was.* I did so long to be with you but had to stop on the way. And you? Will you be all right? Yes, I know, *expected,* but still I could be some use in making the necessary arrangements? I'm at Flora Goforth's place, but if you could send a car to pick me up I could— Oh?— Oh?— Well, Madelyn, all I can say is *accept* it.— Bless you, goodbye. *Accept* it.

[MRS. GOFORTH *is shaken. She moves to the table as if she had received a personal shock.* CHRIS *comes back out. At the same moment, church bells ring in a village below the mountain.*]

CHRIS: —Church bells? In the village?

MRS. GOFORTH: Yes, appropriate, aren't they? Ringing right on a dead cue . . .

CHRIS: I just received news that's—*shocked* me. . . .

MRS. GOFORTH: Another name you have to scratch off the list?

CHRIS: Did you say "list"?

MRS. GOFORTH [*smiling at him cunningly, fiercely*]: I went to a spiritualist once. She said to me, "I hear many dead voices calling, 'Flora, Flora.'" I knew she was a fake, then, since all

92

my close friends call me Sissy. I said, "Tell them to mind their own business, play their gold harps and mind their own harp-playing. Sissy Goforth's not ready to go forth yet and won't go forth till she's ready. . . ."

[CHRIS *extends a hand to her. The bells stop ringing.*]

What are you reaching out for?

CHRIS: Your hand, if I may, Mrs. Goforth. [*He has taken hold of it.*]

MRS. GOFORTH: Hold it but don't squeeze it. The rings cut my fingers.

CHRIS: I'm glad we've talked so frankly, so quickly today. The conversation we had at the ball at the Waldorf in 1950 was a long conversation but not as deep as this one.

MRS. GOFORTH: Who said anything deep? I don't say anything deep in a conversation, not this summer, I save it for my memoirs. Did you say anything deep, in your opinion? If you did, it escaped me, escaped my notice completely. Oh, you've known Swanees. Excuse me, Swamis. You've been exposed to the—intellectual scene, and it's rubbed off on you a little, but only skin-deep, as deep as your little blond beard. . . .

CHRIS: Perhaps I used the wrong word.

[*She places a cigarette in her mouth and waits for him to light it. He turns deliberately away from her, and places a foot on the low balustrade, facing seaward.*]

This "wine-dark sea," it's the oldest sea in the world. . . . Know what I see down there?

MRS. GOFORTH: The sea.

CHRIS: Yes, and a fleet of Roman triremes, those galleys with three banks of oars, rowed by slaves, commanded by commanders headed for conquests. Out for loot. *Boom!* Out for

93

conquering, pillaging, and collecting more slaves. *Boom!* Here's where the whole show started, it's the oldest sea in the Western world, Mrs. Goforth, this sea called the Mediterranean Sea, which means the middle of the earth, was the cradle, of life, not the grave, but the cradle of pagan and Christian—civilizations, this sea, and its connecting river, that old water snake, the Nile.

MRS. GOFORTH: I've been on the Nile. No message. Couple of winters ago I stayed at the Mena House, that hotel under the pyramids. I could see the pyramids, those big-big calcified fools-caps from my breakfast balcony. No message. Rode up to 'em on a camel so I could say I'd done the whole bit.

CHRIS: No message?

MRS. GOFORTH: No message, except you can get seasick on a camel. Yep, you can get mighty seasick on the hump of a camel. Went inside those old king-size tombstones.

CHRIS: No message inside them, either?

MRS. GOFORTH: No message, except the Pharaohs and their families had the idiotic idea they were going to wake up hungry and thirsty and so provided themselves with breakfasts which had gone very stale and dry, and the Pharaohs and families were still sound asleep, ho ho. . . .

[*He still has his back to her. She is obviously annoyed by his loss of attention.*]

And if you look this way, you'll notice I've got a cigarette in my mouth and I'm waiting for you to light it. Didn't that old Sally Ferguson bitch teach you to light a cigarette for a lady?

CHRIS [*facing her*]: She wasn't a bitch, unless all old dying ladies are bitches. She was dying, and scared to death of dying, which made her a little—eccentric . . .

94

[*He has picked up* MRS. GOFORTH's *diamond-studded lighter. He lights her cigarette but doesn't return the lighter to the table. He tosses it in the palm of his hand.*]

MRS. GOFORTH: Thanks. Now put it down.

[*He sits down, smiling, on the low balustrade. There has occurred a marked change in his surface attitude toward her: the deferential air has gone completely.*]

I meant my Bulgari lighter, not your—*backside!*

[*He studies the lighter as if to calculate its value. There is a pause.*]

If you don't put that lighter back down on the table, I'm going to call for Rudy! You know Rudy. You've made his acquaintance, I think.

CHRIS: If I don't put it down on the table but in my pocket, and if I were to run down the goatpath with it—how fast can Rudy run?

MRS. GOFORTH: How fast can *you* run? Could you outrun the dogs? Yesterday you didn't outrun the dogs.

CHRIS: That was—uphill, on the other side of your mountain. I think I could get down this side, yes, by the—funicular, I could operate it.

MRS. GOFORTH: Can you outrun a bullet?

CHRIS: Oh, would you have Rudy shoot at me for this lighter.

MRS. GOFORTH: You bet I would. That's a very valuable lighter.

[CHRIS *laughs and tosses the lighter on the table.*]

CHRIS: Hmmm. On a parapet over the Western world's oldest sea, the lady that owns it had a gangster—

MRS. GOFORTH: The bodyguard of a syndicate gangster!

CHRIS: Yes, the lady that owns it had her bodyguard shoot down a—what?—burnt-out poet who had confiscated a diamond-studded lighter because he was unfed and hungry. He'd been on a five-day fast for—nonsecular reasons, and it had upset his reason.

[MRS. GOFORTH *rings the bell on the table.* CHRIS *seizes her hand and wrests the bell away from it. She rises from the table and shouts: "Rudy!"*]

CHRIS [*louder than she*]: Rudy!

MRS. GOFORTH: You couldn't get away with it!

CHRIS: Oh, yes, I could, if I wanted. [*He tosses the bell back on the table with a mocking grin.*]

MRS. GOFORTH: What a peculiar—puzzlesome young man you are! You came out here like a dandy, kissed my hand, and now you're coming on like a young hood all of a sudden, and I don't like the change, it makes me nervous with you, and now I don't know if I want you around here or not, or if I'm—not superstitious. See? You've made me shaky.

CHRIS: You didn't know I was teasing?

MRS. GOFORTH: No. You're too good at it.

CHRIS: [*looking seaward*]: I see it, your oubliette on the beach, it looks attractive to me.

MRS. GOFORTH: Help me into my bedroom. [*She tries to rise but falls back into the chair.*] It's time for my siesta.

CHRIS: Could I stay there, a while?

MRS. GOFORTH: Later maybe. Not now. I need to rest.

96

CHRIS: I meant the grass hut on the beach, not your bedroom.

MRS. GOFORTH: Be still, she's coming back out, my secretary, and I'm not sure I trust her.

CHRIS: Do you trust anybody?

MRS. GOFORTH: Nobody human, just dogs. All except poodles, I never trusted a poodle. . . .

[BLACKIE *comes onto the terrace.*]

In again, out again, Finnegan! What's it *this* time, Blackie?

BLACKIE: Is it true you've discharged the kitchen staff again, Mrs. Goforth?

MRS. GOFORTH: Yes, it's true. . . . Haven't you heard about the inventory?

BLACKIE: What inventory, inventory of what?

MRS. GOFORTH: I had an intuition that things were disappearing and had Rudy check my list of fabulous china, my Sèvres, Limoges, Lowestoff, against what was still on the mountain. Half of it gone, decimated! And my Medici silver, banquet silver used by the Medicis hundreds of years ago, *gone!*—That's what the inventory disclosed!

BLACKIE: Mrs. Goforth, is it possible you don't remember—

MRS. GOFORTH: *What?*

BLACKIE: You had it removed to a storage house in Naples, in an armored truck.

MRS. GOFORTH: *Me?*

BLACKIE: *You!*

MRS. GOFORTH: *Not true!*

97

BLACKIE: Mrs. Goforth, when people are very ill and taking drugs for it, they get confused, their memories are confused, they get delusions.

MRS. GOFORTH: *This mountain has been systematically pillaged!* — That's what the inventory—

BLACKIE: An inventory made by the bodyguard of a syndicate gangster?

MRS. GOFORTH: How dare you suggest— *I have a guest at the table!*

BLACKIE: *I will always dare to say what I know to be true!*

MRS. GOFORTH: *Go in, find my checkbook and write out a check for yourself for whatever's coming to you, and bring it out here and I'll sign it for cash, at the Naples branch of my bank! You wanted out, now you got it, so take it! Take it!*

BLACKIE: *Gladly! Gladly!*

MRS. GOFORTH: Mutually *gladly! Go in!*

[BLACKIE *starts to go.* MRS. GOFORTH'S *shouting has brought on a coughing spasm. She covers her mouth with her hands and rushes, in a crouched position, toward the upstage area of the library.*]

CHRIS: *—Boom* . . .

BLACKIE: *Release!*

CHRIS [*pointing at the terrace pavement*]: Blackie? Look!— Blood, she's bleeding. . . .

MRS. GOFORTH'S VOICE [*Off stage, hoarsely*]: *Dottore, chiama il dottore! Giulio, Simonetta!*

CHRIS: You'd better go in there with her.

98

BLACKIE: I can't yet. They'll get the doctor for her. [*She moves downstage, gasping.*] You see, she's made me *inhuman!*

[SIMONETTA *explodes onto the forestage.*]

SIMONETTA: *Signorina, la Signora é molto, molto malata!*

BLACKIE [*going toward her*]: *Dov'è la Signora, in camera da letto?*

SIMONETTA: *No, nella biblioteca, con il dottore!* [*She sits on a bench and sobs hysterically.*]

BLACKIE: Well, I'd better go in there.

CHRIS: What shall I do? Anything?

BLACKIE: Yes, stay here, don't go. [*Then, to* SIMONETTA, *who is now crying theatrically*] *Ferma questa—commedia.*

[SIMONETTA *stops crying, and begins straightening up the table.*]

[*To* CHRIS] Call the hospital in Rome, Salvatore Mundi, and ask for Dr. Rengucci. Tell him what's happening here and a nurse is needed at once. Then come in there, the library, and we'll—

[GIULIO *rushes out onto the forestage.*]

GIULIO: *La Signora Goforth vuol' vedere il Signore, presto, molto presto!*

BLACKIE [*to* CHRIS]: She's calling for *you.* I'd better go in first. Make the call and then come to the library.

[*She goes out one way,* CHRIS *the other.*]

GIULIO [*to* SIMONETTA]: She's dying?

SIMONETTA: No one's been paid this week. Who will pay us if she dies today?

GIULIO: *Guarda!*

[*He shows her a gold bracelet.* SIMONETTA *snatches at it.* GIULIO *pockets it with a grin, and starts off as she follows.*]

THE SCENE DIMS OUT.

SCENE SIX

Later the same day, toward sundown. The interiors of the white villa are screened and the terrace is lighted more coolly. BLACKIE *is seated at the downstage table, jotting in a notebook memoranda of things to be done before leaving. The* STAGE ASSISTANTS *stand by the flagstaff ready to lower the banner of* MRS. GOFORTH.

ONE: Cable her daughter that the old bitch is dying.

TWO: The banner of the griffin is about to be lowered.

BLACKIE [*as if translating their speech into a polite paraphrase*]: Cable Mrs. Goforth's daughter at Point Goforth, Long Island, that her mother is not expected to survive the night, and I'm waiting for—immediate—instructions.

ONE: Fireworks tonight at Point Goforth, Long Island.

TWO: A champagne fountain.

ONE *and* TWO [*together*]: Death: celebration.

BLACKIE: Call police in Amalfi to guard the library safe till Rudy has gone.

ONE: Rudy's root-a-toot-tooting through that safe right now.

TWO: He's disappointed to discover that the old bitch still has on her most important jewels.

ONE: And she's still conscious—fiercely!

BLACKIE: Contact mortuary. Amalfi.

TWO: That Blackie's a cool one.

[CHRIS *comes onto the terrace, now wearing his repaired lederhosen and a washed, but unironed, white shirt.*]

CHRIS: Blackie?

BLACKIE [*glancing up*]: Oh. I'm making out a list of things to do before leaving.

CHRIS: You're not leaving right away, are you?

BLACKIE: Soon as I get instructions from her daughter.

CHRIS: I called the Rome doctor and told him what had happened. He said he's expected it sooner, and there's nothing more to be done that can't be done by the doctor on the place.

BLACKIE: The little doctor, Lullo, has given her a strong shot of adrenalin which was a mistake, I think. She won't go to bed, keeps pressing electric buzzers for Simonetta who's run away, and she's put on all her rings so they won't be stolen. She's more afraid of being robbed of her jewelry than her life. What time would it be in the States?

CHRIS: What time is it here?

BLACKIE: Sundown, nearly.

CHRIS: About seven-thirty here would make it—about two-thirty there.

BLACKIE: Maybe a phone call would get through before a cable.

[*She rises. One of the* STAGE ASSISTANTS *brings a phone from the table by the chaise lounge, a little upstage.* BLACKIE *takes the phone.*

Try her daughter's husband at Goforth, Faller and Rush, Incorporated, Plaza 1-9000, while I—

[*She gives* CHRIS *the phone, and pours herself a brandy.* RUDY *comes out with a strongbox from the safe.*]

Who's that? Oh! *You!* What are you taking out?

RUDY: Just what I was told to take out.

BLACKIE: Well, take it out, but don't forget that everything's been listed.

RUDY: I don't forget nothing, Blackie. [*He goes off.*]

STAGE ASSISTANT ONE [*removing the crested screen*]: Her bedroom in the white villa.

TWO: The griffin is staring at death, and trying to outstare it.

[*We see* MRS. GOFORTH *seated. She wears a majestic ermine-trimmed robe to which she has pinned her "most important jewels," and rings blaze on her fingers that clench the chair arms.*]

ONE: Her eyes are bright as her diamonds.

TWO: Until she starts bleeding again, she'll give no ground to any real or suspected adversary. . . .

ONE: And *then?*

[*During this exchange between the* ASSISTANTS, *who now back into the wings on their soundless shoes,* BLACKIE *has made several other notations. Without looking up at* CHRIS, *she asks him:*]

BLACKIE: You're still very hungry, aren't you?

CHRIS: Yes, very.

BLACKIE: The new kitchen staff has arrived. I've put a bottle of milk in your rucksack, and your rucksack is in the library. You'd better just have the milk now. We'll have dinner later together.

CHRIS: Blackie, I've seen her grass hut on the beach, her oubliette, as she calls it. And—I wonder how long I could stay down there before I'd be discovered and—evicted?

103

BLACKIE: Long as you want to. Indefinitely, I guess. But how would you live down there with the villas all closed?

CHRIS: Oh, on—*frutti di mare:* shellfish. And I'd make a spear for spear-fishing.

BLACKIE: There's no fresh water down there, just the sea water.

CHRIS: I know how to make fresh water out of sea water.

BLACKIE: Why would you want to stay down there?

CHRIS [*as a wave crashes under the mountain*]: Boom! I'd like to make a mobile. I'd call it "Boom." The sea and the sky are turning the same color, dissolving into each other. Wine-dark sea and wine-dark sky. In a little while the little fishing boats with their lamps for night fishing will make the sea look like the night sky turned upside down, and you and I will have a sort of valedictory dinner on the terrace.

BLACKIE: Yes, it sounds very peaceful. . . .

[*The bedroom of the white villa is now brightened.* MRS. GOFORTH *staggers from her chair, knocking it over. The* STAGE ASSISTANTS *dart out to snatch the small chair and move it farther away, as she leans on a bed post, gasping. Then she draws herself up, advances to the chair's new position a little farther back. She reaches out for it. The* ASSISTANTS *pull it farther. She staggers dizzily after it. The* ASSISTANTS *exchange inquiring looks. They silently agree to allow her the chair and they back out of the area. She sits down with a cry of fury and resumes her fierce contest with death. A reserve of power, triggered by the adrenalin, begins to reanimate her. She rises and drags the chair to a small boudoir table and calls out:*]

MRS. GOFORTH: *Chris? Chris?*

BLACKIE: That's her, she's calling for you. Can you stand to go in there?

104

CHRIS: Sure I can—it's a professional duty.

[*As he turns upstage, the* STAGE ASSISTANTS *remove the screen masking the library. He enters that area. One of the* STAGE ASSISTANTS *turns the screen perpendicular to the proscenium so that it represents a wall division between bedroom and library. They retire.*]

Boom! Mrs. Goforth?

MRS. GOFORTH: Oh, you've finally got here. Stay out there, don't come in here right away. The doctor gave me a shot that's made me a little dizzy, I'll call you in—in a minute. . . . [*She staggers up from the chair, knocking it over.*]

CHRIS: Are you all right, Mrs. Goforth? [*He discovers his sack, removes and opens the milk bottle.*]

MRS. GOFORTH: Just a little unsteady after the shot, the doctor said. The bleeding was from a little blood vessel at the back of my throat. But he thinks I ought to lay off the work for a while, just wind up this volume and save the rest for—sequels. . . .

[CHRIS *opens the milk bottle and sips the milk as if it were sacramental wine.*]

Don't you think that's better, since it's such a strain on me?

CHRIS: Yes, I do, I think it's a—[*drinks milk*]—a wise decision. . . . [*He catches some drops of milk that have run down his chin, licks them almost reverently off the palm of his hand.*]

MRS. GOFORTH [*entering the library*]: All that work, the pressure, was burning me up, it was literally burning me up like a house on fire.

CHRIS [*assisting her to the desk chair*]: Yes, we—all live in a house on fire, no fire department to call; no way out, just the upstairs window to look out of while the fire burns the house down with us trapped, locked in it.

105

MRS. GOFORTH: What do you mean by—what windows?

CHRIS [*touching his forehead*]: These upstairs windows, not wide enough to crawl out of, just wide enough to lean out of and look out of, and—look and look and look, till we're almost nothing but looking, nothing, almost, but *vision*. . . .

MRS. GOFORTH: Hmmm.— Yes. It isn't as cool out here as it was in my bedroom and this robe I've put on is too heavy. So come ·on in. We can talk in my bedroom. [*She retires behind the bedroom screen.*]

MRS. GOFORTH'S VOICE [*from behind her screen*]: Talking between rooms is a strain on the ears and the vocal cords—so come in, now: I'm ready.

[*He crosses to the screens, stops short.*]

CHRIS: Oh. Sorry. [*He turns away from the screens.*] I'll wait till you've—

MRS. GOFORTH'S VOICE: Modesty? *Modesty?* I wouldn't expect you to suffer from modesty, Chris. I never was bothered with silliness of that kind. If you've got a figure that's pleasing to look at, why be selfish with it?

CHRIS: Yes, it *was* a pleasure, Mrs. Goforth.

MRS. GOFORTH'S VOICE: Then why'd you retreat, back away? In my bedroom, in here, I almost never, if ever, wear a stitch of clothes in summer. I like to feel cool air on my bare skin in summer. Don't you like that? Cool air and cool water on the bare skin in summer's the nicest thing about summer. Huh? Don't you think so, too?

CHRIS: I've found my duffel bag. It wandered in here, for some reason.

MRS. GOFORTH'S VOICE: I had it brought there so I could get

106

your passport for the local police. They want a look at the passport of anyone just arrived.

CHRIS: I see.

MRS. GOFORTH'S VOICE: You'll get it back when you go, you know, there's no hurry, is there?

CHRIS: I'm not sure about that. [*Finds passport.*] Anyway, it's already been returned.

MRS. GOFORTH: We've just been getting acquainted. The preliminaries of a friendship, or any kind of relationship, are the most difficult part, and our talk on the terrace was just a—preliminary.

CHRIS [*wryly, so low that she cannot hear*]: Sometimes the preliminaries are rougher than the main bout. [*He is rearranging articles in the rucksack.*]

MRS. GOFORTH: I didn't catch that. What was that?

CHRIS [*to himself*]: I didn't mean you to catch it.

MRS. GOFORTH: Stop mumbling and fussing with that metal stuff in the sack. The fussing drowns out the mumbling. D'ya want me to break another blood vessel in my throat talking to you from here?

CHRIS: Are you dressed now, Mrs. Goforth?

MRS. GOFORTH: Hell, I told you I'm never dressed in my bedroom.

CHRIS: You said "rarely if ever"—not "never." [*He sighs and crosses to the door again.*] You have a beautiful body, Mrs. Goforth. It's a privilege to be permitted to admire it. It makes me think of one of those great fountain figures in Scandinavian countries.

MRS. GOFORTH: Yeah, well, baby, a fountain figure is a stone figure and my body isn't a stone figure, although it's been sculpted by several world-famous sculptors, it's still a flesh and blood figure. And don't think it's been easy to keep it the way it still is. I'm going to lie down and rest now on this cool bed. Mmmm, these sheets are so cool—come on in. Why are you standing there paralyzed in that door?

CHRIS: I'm—silent on a peak in—Darien. . . . [*Turns away from the door.*] I came here hoping to be your friend, Mrs. Goforth, but—

MRS. GOFORTH'S VOICE: You said "but" something, but what?

CHRIS: I wouldn't have come here unless I thought I was able to serve some purpose or other, in return for a temporary refuge, a place to rest and work in, where I could get back that sense of reality I've been losing lately, as I tried to explain on the terrace, but— [*He has removed the large mobile under her desk. He climbs on the desk to attach the mobile to the chandelier above it.*] You knew I was hungry but it was "black coffee or else."

MRS. GOFORTH: Is that why you won't come in here?

CHRIS: It would just be embarrasing for us both if I did. [*He jumps off the desk.*]

MRS. GOFORTH: *What's that, what're you doing?*

CHRIS: I hung up a gift I brought you, a mobile called "The Earth Is a Wheel in a Great Big Gambling Casino." And now I think I should leave, I have a long way to go.

MRS. GOFORTH: Just a minute. I'm coming back out there to see this mobile of yours. [*She comes from behind the screen, pulling the regal white robe about her.*] Well, where is it?

CHRIS: Right over your head.

108

[*She looks up, staggering against the desk.*]

MRS. GOFORTH: It doesn't move, doesn't go.

CHRIS: It will, when it's caught by the wind.

[*The mobile begins to turn, casting faint flickers of light.*]

There now, the winds caught it, it's turning. [*He picks up his canvas sack, preparing to leave.*]

MRS. GOFORTH: [*picking up the phone, suddenly*]: Kitchen, *cucina, cucina!— Cucina? Un momento!* [*She thrusts the phone toward* CHRIS.] Tell the cook what you would like for supper.

CHRIS: Anything, Mrs. Goforth.

MRS. GOFORTH [*into the phone*]: O.K.— *Cucina? Senta— Pranzo questa sera.— Pastina in brodo, per cominciare. Capish?— Si!— Poi, una grande pesca, si, si, una grandissima pesca, anche— carne freddo, si, si, carne freddo—* Roast Beef, Bif, Beeeeeef! [*Gasps, catches her breath.*] *Prosciutto, legumi, tutti, tutti legumi Capito? Poi, un' insalata verde. No, Mista! Insalata mista, Mista!* They don't know their own language. . . . *Poi, dolce, zuppa inglese, frutta, formaggio, tutte formaggio, e vino, vino, bianco e rosso, una bottiglia di Soave e una bottiglia di—* [*gasps for breath again.*] *Valpolicella. Hanh?— Va bene.* . . . [*hangs up.*] This new cook sounds like a—Mau-mau. . . . She'll probably serve us long pig with—shrunk heads on toothpicks stuck in it. . . . [*She tries to laugh, but coughs.*] Now, then, you see, you're not just going to be fed, you're going to be wined and dined in high style tonight on the terrace. But meanwhile, we're going to enjoy a long siesta together in the cool of my bedroom which is full of historical treasures, including myself! [*She crosses to the bedroom doors, beckons him commandingly. He doesn't move.*] Well?!

CHRIS: I'm afraid I came here too late to accept these—invitations.

MRS. GOFORTH: Who else has invited you somewhere?

CHRIS: I've passed the point where I wait for invitations, but I think I'll be welcomed by the elderly spinster lady whose mother died in Taormina today.

MRS. GOFORTH: Not if she's heard your nickname. And Sicily's an island. How'll you get there, can you walk on water?

CHRIS: Your discharged secretary gave me a bottle of milk with some ten thousand lire notes attached to it with a— rubber band. So—goodbye, Mrs. Goforth. [*He bends to hoist his rucksack over his shoulder.*]

MRS. GOFORTH: Mr. Flanders, you have the distinction, the dubious distinction, of being the first man that wouldn't come into my bedroom when invited to enter.

CHRIS: I'm sorry.

MRS. GOFORTH: Man bring this up road, huh? [*She has snatched up his book of poems.*]

CHRIS: No, I—

MRS. GOFORTH: What else? Your book of poems, your calling card? Y'must be running short of 'em. Here take it back! [*She hurls it at his feet.*] I haven't read it but I can imagine the contents. *Facile sentiment!* To be good a poem's got to be tough and to write a good, tough poem you've got to cut your teeth on the marrow bone of this world. I think you're still cutting your milk teeth, Mr. Flanders.

CHRIS: I know you better than you know me. I admire you, admire you so much I almost like you, *almost.* I think if that old Greek explorer, Pytheas, hadn't beat you to it by centuries, you would've sailed up through the Gates of Hercules to map out the Western world, and you would have sailed up farther and mapped it out better than he did. No storm could've driven you

110

back or changed your course. Oh, no, you're nobody's fool, but you're a fool, Mrs. Goforth, if you don't know that finally, sooner or later, you need somebody or something to mean God to you, even if it's a cow on the streets of Bombay, or carved rock on the Easter Islands or—

MRS. GOFORTH: You came here to bring me *God*, did you?

CHRIS: I didn't say God, I said someone or something to—

MRS. GOFORTH: I heard what you said, you said *God*. My eyes are out of focus but not my ears! Well, *bring* Him, I'm ready to lay out a red carpet for Him, but how do you bring Him? Whistle? Ring a bell for Him? [*She snatches a bell off her desk and rings it fiercely.*] Huh? How? What? [*She staggers back against the desk, gasping.*]

CHRIS: I've failed, I've disappointed some people in what they wanted or thought they wanted from me, Mrs. Goforth, but sometimes, once in a while, I've given them what they needed even if they didn't know what it was. I brought it up the road to them, and that's how I got the name that's made me unwelcome this summer.

STAGE ASSISTANT ONE: Tell her about the first time!

STAGE ASSISTANTS [*together*]: Tell her, tell her, the first time!

[*They draw back to the wings. Music begins to be heard softly*].

CHRIS: —I was at Mrs. Ferguson's mountain above Palm Springs, the first time. I wasn't used to her world of elegant bitches and dandies. . . . Early one morning I went down the mountain and across the desert on a walking trip to a village in Baja California, where a great Hindu teacher had gathered a group of pupils, disciples, about him. Along the road I passed a rest home that looked like a grand hotel, and just a little farther along, I came to an inlet, an estuary of the ocean, and I stopped

111

for a swim off the beach that was completely deserted. Swam out in the cool water till my head felt cool as the water, then turned and swam back in, but the beach wasn't deserted completely any more. There was a very old gentleman on it. He called "Help!" to me, as if he was in the water drowning, and I was on the shore. I swam in and asked him how I could help him and he said this, he said: "Help me out there! I can't make it alone, I've gone past pain I can bear." I could see it was true. He was elegantly dressed but emaciated, cadaverous. I gave him the help he wanted, I led him out in the water, it wasn't easy. Once he started to panic; I had to hold onto him tight as a lover till he got back his courage and said, "All right." The tide took him as light as a leaf. But just before I did that, and this is the oddest thing, he took out his wallet and thrust all the money in it into my hand. Here take this, he said to me. And I—

MRS. GOFORTH: Took it, did you, you took it?

CHRIS: The sea had no use for his money. The fish in the sea had no use for it, either, so I took it and went on where I was going.

MRS. GOFORTH: How much were you paid for this—service?

CHRIS: It was a very special difficult service. I was well paid for it.

MRS. GOFORTH: Did you tell the old Hindu, the Swami, when you got to his place, that you'd killed an old man on the way and—

CHRIS: I told him that I had helped a dying old man to get through it.

MRS. GOFORTH: What did he say about that?

CHRIS [*reflectively*]: What did he say?— He said, "You've found your vocation," and he smiled. It was a beautiful smile in spite of showing bare gums, and—he held out his hand for the money. The hand was beautiful, too, in spite of being dry skin, pulled tight as a glove, over bones.

MRS. GOFORTH: Did you give him the money?

CHRIS: Yes, they needed the money. I didn't. I gave it to them.

MRS. GOFORTH: I *bet* you did.

CHRIS: I *did*.

MRS. GOFORTH: Did he say thank you for it?

CHRIS: I don't know if he did. You see, they— No, I guess you don't see. They had a belief in believing that too much is said, when feeling, quiet feelings—enough—says more. . . .

And he had a gift for gesture. You couldn't believe how a hand that shriveled and splotched could make such a beautiful gesture of holding out the hand to be helped up from the ground. It made me, so quickly, peaceful. That was important to me, that sudden feeling of quiet, because I'd come there, all the way down there, with the—the spectre of lunacy at my heels all the way— He said: "Stay."— We sat about a fire on the beach that night: Nobody said anything.

MRS. GOFORTH: No message, he didn't have any message?

CHRIS: Yes, that night it was silence, it was the meaning of silence.

MRS. GOFORTH: Silence? Meaning?

CHRIS: Acceptance.

MRS. GOFORTH: What of?

CHRIS: Oh, many things, everything, nearly. Such as how to live and to die in a way that's more dignified than most of us know how to do it. And of how not to be frightened of not knowing what isn't meant to be known, acceptance of not knowing *anything* but the moment of still existing, until we stop existing—and acceptance of that moment, too.

MRS. GOFORTH: How do you know he wasn't just an old faker?

CHRIS: How do you know that I'm not just a young one?

MRS. GOFORTH: I don't. You *are* what they call you!

CHRIS [*taking hold of her hand*]: As much as *anyone* is what anyone calls him.

MRS. GOFORTH: A butcher is called a butcher, and that's what he is. A baker is called a baker, and he's a baker. A—

CHRIS: Whatever they're called, they're men, and being *men*, they're not known by themselves or anyone else.

MRS. GOFORTH: [*presses a button that shrills on the stage*]: Rudy? Rudy!

CHRIS: Your bodyguard's gone, Mrs. Goforth.

[*She goes on pressing the button.*]

He left with the contents of your strongbox, your safe.

MRS. GOFORTH: —I've got on me all my important jewels, and if Rudy's gone, I want you to go, too. Go on to your next appointment. You've tired me, you've done me in. This day has been the most awful day of my life. . . .

CHRIS: I know. That's why you need me here a while longer.

[*He places his arm about her.*]

MRS. GOFORTH: *Don't, don't.* You—*scare* me!

CHRIS: Let me take you into your bedroom, now, and put you to bed, Mrs. Goforth.

MRS. GOFORTH: *No, no,* GO. *Let me* GO!!

[*He releases her and picks up his canvas sack.*]

114

Hey!

[*He pauses with his back to her.*]

Did somebody tell you I was dying this summer? Yes, isn't that why you came here, because you imagined that I'd be ripe for a soft touch because I'm dying this summer? Come on, for once in your life be honestly frank, be frankly honest with someone! You've been tipped off that old Flora Goforth is about to go forth this summer.

CHRIS: Yes, that's why I came here.

MRS. GOFORTH: Well, I've escorted four husbands to the eternal threshold, and come back alone without them, just with the loot of *three* of them, and, ah, God, it was like I was building a shell of bone round my heart with their goddamn loot, their loot the material for it— It's my turn, now, to go forth, and I've got no choice but to do it. But I'll do it alone. I don't want to be escorted. I want to go forth alone. But you, you counted on touching my heart because you'd heard I was dying, and old dying people are your specialty, your vocation. But you miscalculated wth this one. This milk train doesn't stop here anymore. I'll give you some practical advice. Go back to Naples. Walk along Santa Lucia, the bay-front. Yesterday, there, they smelt the smell of no money, and treated you like a used, discarded used person. It'll be different this time. You'll probably run into some Americans at a sidewalk table along there, a party that's in for some shopping from the islands. If you're lucky, they'll ask you to sit down with them and say, "Won't you have something, Chris?"— Well, *have* something, Chris! and if you play your cards right, they might invite you to go back to an island with them. Your best bet is strangers, I guess. Don't work on the young ones or anybody attractive. They're not ripe to be taken. And not the old ones, either, they've been taken too often. Work on the middle-aged drunks, that's who to work on, Chris, work on them. Sometimes the old milk train still comes to

115

a temporary stop at their crazy station, so concentrate on the middle-aged drunks in Naples.

CHRIS: This isn't the time for such—practical advice. . . .

[*She makes a gasping sound and presses a tissue to her mouth, turning away.*]

MRS. GOFORTH: [*facing front*]: —A paper rose . . . [*The tissue is dyed red with blood.*] Before you go, help me into my bedroom, I can't make it alone. . . .

[*He conducts her to the screen between the two rooms as the* STAGE ASSISTANTS *advance from the wings to remove it.*]

—It's full of historical treasures. The chandelier, if the dealer that sold it to me wasn't a liar, used to hang in Versailles, and the bed, if he wasn't lying, was the bed of Countess Walewska, Napoleon's Polish mistress. It's a famous old bed, for a famous old body. . . .

[*The* STAGE ASSISTANTS *remove the screen masking the bed.*]

CHRIS: Yes, it looks like the catafalque of an Empress. [*He lifts her onto the bed, and draws a cover over her.*]

MRS. GOFORTH: *Don't leave me alone till—*

CHRIS: I never leave till the end.

[*She blindly stretches out her jeweled hand. He takes it.*]

MRS. GOFORTH: —*Not so tight, the—*

CHRIS: I know, the rings cut your fingers.

[*He draws a ring off a finger. She gasps. He draws off another. She gasps again.*]

MRS. GOFORTH: Be here, when I wake up.

[*The* STAGE ASSISTANTS *place before her bed the screen with the gold-winged griffin on the middle panel. Light dims out on that area, and is brought up on the turning mobile. Music seems to come from the turning mobile that casts very delicate gleams of light on the stage.* BLACKIE *appears on the forestage as the* STAGE ASSISTANTS *bring out a dinner table and rapidly set two places. Then they cross to the flagstaff by the right wings and begin slowly to lower the flag.*]

ONE: Flag-lowering ceremony on the late Mrs. Goforth's mountain.

TWO: Bugle?

[*A muted bugle is heard from a distance.*]

That's not Taps, that's Reveille.

ONE: It's Reveille always, Taps never, for the gold griffin.

TWO: One more obvious statement is one too many. [*He snaps his fingers.*] Let's go.

[*They go out with the folded banner.* CHRIS *comes from behind the bedroom screen, onto the terrace where* BLACKIE *sits coolly waiting. She rises and pours wine into a medieval goblet as she speaks to* CHRIS.]

BLACKIE: —Is it—is she—?

[CHRIS *nods as he moves out onto the forestage.*]

Was it what they call "peaceful"?

[CHRIS *nods again.*]

With all that fierce life in her?

CHRIS: You always wonder afterwards where it's gone, so far, so quickly. You feel it must be still around somewhere, in the air. But there's no sign of it.

117

BLACKIE: Did she say anything to you before she—?

CHRIS: She said to me: "Be here when I wake up." After I'd taken her hand and stripped the rings off her fingers.

BLACKIE: What did you do with—?

CHRIS [*giving her a quick look that might suggest an understandable shrewdness*]: Under her pillow like a Pharaoh's breakfast waiting for the Pharaoh to wake up hungry. . . .

[BLACKIE *comes up beside him on the forestage and offers him the wine goblet. A wave is heard breaking under the mountain.*]

BLACKIE: The sea is saying the name of your next mobile.

CHRIS: *Boom!*

BLACKIE: What does it mean?

CHRIS: It says "Boom" and that's what it means. No translation, no explanation, just "Boom." [*He drinks from the goblet and passes it back to her.*]

THE CURTAIN FALLS SLOWLY.